# LEIBSTANDARTE
## ARDENNES 1944–45

Steven Smith

PHILADELPHIA & OXFORD

Published in the United States of America and Great Britain in 2016 by CASEMATE PUBLISHERS
1950 Lawrence Road, Havertown, PA 19083
and 10 Hythe Bridge Street, Oxford, OX1 2EW

Copyright 2017 © Simon Forty

ISBN-13: 978-1-61200-542-3

Produced by Greene Media Ltd.

Cataloging-in-publication data is available from the Library of Congress and the British Library.

All rights reserved. With the exception of quoting brief passages for the purposes of review, no part of this publication may be reproduced, stored in a retrieval system, or transmitted in any form or by any means, electronic, mechanical, photocopying, recording, or otherwise without prior written permission from the Publisher.

The information in this book is true and complete to the best of our knowledge. All recommendations are made without any guarantee on the part of the Authors or Publisher, who also disclaim any liability incurred in connection with the use of this data or specific details.

All Internet site information provided was correct when received from the Authors. The Publisher can accept no responsibility for this information becoming incorrect.

10 9 8 7 6 5 4 3 2 1

Printed and bound in China
For a complete list of Casemate titles please contact:
CASEMATE PUBLISHERS (US)
Telephone (610) 853-9131, Fax (610) 853-9146
E-mail: casemate@casematepublishers.com

CASEMATE PUBLISHERS (UK)
Telephone (01865) 241249, Fax (01865) 794449
E-mail: casemate-uk@casematepublishers.co.uk

### Acknowledgments
Most of the original photos come from NARA, College Park, or BattlefieldHistorian.com. The aerial photography is by Leo Marriott; other land-based modern material was taken by Richard Wood or Simon Forty unless credited otherwise. If anyone is missing or incorrectly credited, apologies: please notify the author through the publishers.

We'd like to thank in particular Leo Marriott, Mark Franklin (as usual the excellent maps), Ian Hughes (design concept), Richard Wood (driving) and the military cyclists (particularly Peter Anderson) for photos and enthusiasm.

Finally, it is impossible to produce a book like this without acknowledging the work of Jean Paul Pallud, particularly *Battle of the Bulge Then and Now*, and its publisher After the Battle: brilliant and seminal.

**Previous page:**
Classic Battle of the Bulge. The photos show KG Hansen at Poteau (see page 38).

**This Page:**
The December weather favored the attackers initially as snow and fog kept Allied aircraft grounded.

**Abbreviations**

**AAA** Antiaircraft artillery
**CCA/B/R** Combat Command A/B/ Reserve
**CP** Command post
**ECB** Engineer combat battalion
**ETHINT** European Theater Historical Interrogations
**FJR** Fallschirmjäger (German paras)
**HJ** Hitlerjugend (12th SS-Pz Div)
**KG** Kampfgruppe
**LSSAH** Leibstandarte SS Adolf Hitler (1st SS-Pz Div)
**PIR** Parachute infantry regiment
**RCT** Regimental combat team
**TD** Tank destroyer (tracked or towed artillery)

# Contents

| | | | |
|---|---|---|---|
| Introduction | 4 | KG Knittel | 40 |
| LSSAH history | 12 | December 19 | 42 |
| The Plan | 16 | December 20 | 44 |
| Into Action | 18 | December 21–25 | 50 |
| December 17 | 22 | Aftermath | 60 |
| Malmédy | 28 | Cemeteries | 62 |
| December 18 | 32 | Bibliography | 64 |
| KG Hansen | 38 | Key to Map Symbols | 64 |

# Introduction

**Above:**
Leibstandarte's insignia, the skeleton key, was a play on Sepp Dietrich's name: *Dietrich* means skeleton key or lockpick.

**Below Left:**
Jochen Peiper (at right in overcoat) seen in Russia with tank ace Michael Wittmann and his crew.

**Below Right:**
Max Hansen (1908–90) commanded 12. Company of LSSAH in 1939. By fall 1944 he was a *Standartenführer* (Colonel) commanding the 1st SS-PzGr Regt.

As the end of 1944 approached, Nazi Germany found itself in a vise. Having lost nearly all of its conquered territory, opposing armies were now up to the very gates of the Reich, from both the east and west—not to mention from above, where Allied airpower was raining down bombs on every city or industrial facility they could find.

After the disasters of summer 1944, however, some automatic advantages accrued to the Germans once fall arrived. For one thing, the fast advances of the Soviets and Western Allies had caused them both to outrun their supply lines, while the Germans had only fallen back closer to their own. The fixed defenses of the Reich, such as the Westwall, gave German troops succor, and intelligence resources also improved once on native territory. Even as the last German troops were evacuating France and the Low Countries, and the Soviets had pulled up outside Warsaw, Adolf Hitler was thinking of the counterblow he could launch once Germany had returned to a tightened knot.

He had the wherewithal for one more major blow—seizing back the initiative in either the East or West. If he could defeat one opponent, then he could turn on the other. Hitler decided that his most vulnerable opponent was the Americans—so the last great German offensive of the war would take place in the Ardennes, a scene of German successes in the past, and where for some reason the US still only maintained a thinly held front.

During the fall of 1944, while resisting Eisenhower's "broad front" with stubbornness, the Germans meantime created a strategic reserve. Accustomed to camouflage and concealment by now, the Germans assembled two full panzer armies for a counteroffensive, unknown to Allied intelligence.

The great attack would be led by the 1st SS Panzer Division, Leibstandarte Adolf Hitler, and the spearhead of that division would be led by Joachim Peiper, a 29-year-old with a combat-record second to none in the Wehrmacht. It is fair to consider it understandable that in Hitler's last great offensive of the war he relied foremost on the division that bore his name. It is also clear that, after all its great struggles in Russia and Normandy, the Leibstandarte—now fully re-equipped and rested—was eager to prove itself again. The Ardennes Offensive, or as it is more commonly known, The Battle of the Bulge, would give the Leibstandarte one more chance to strike a telling blow for Germany.

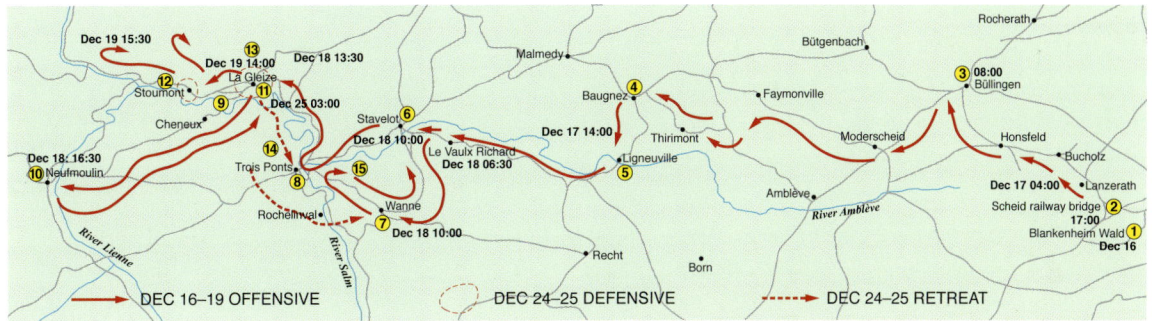

**Above:**

**1** KG Peiper leaves assembly area in Blankenheim Forest; **2** Crosses the Scheid railway bridge; **3** Büllingen fuel dump; **4** Massacre at Baugnez crossroads takes place around 14:30; **5** Peiper just misses Brig. Timberlake; **6** Stavelot bridge crossed—retaken by US forces, fighting continues until December 25; **7** Wanne is taken and Mohnke moves Div HQ here on the 19th; **8** Bridges blown at Trois Ponts (Amblève 11:15; Salm 13:00); **9** Cheneux bridge found intact, air attack c. 14:30; **10** Peiper is stymied at Neufmoulin; **11** Returns to La Gleize where elements of KG Knittel join; **12** Attack though Stoumont and Târgnon held at Stoumont Station; **13** Denouement at La Gleize; **14** Retreat by 800 survivors to Wanne; **15** Petit Spai bridge where the last LSSAH troops north of the Amblève crossed back on Dec 25.

**Below:**

Hitler's plan to regain the initiative in the West, split the Allies and reach Antwerp. It would give him time to turn his full attention toward the East.

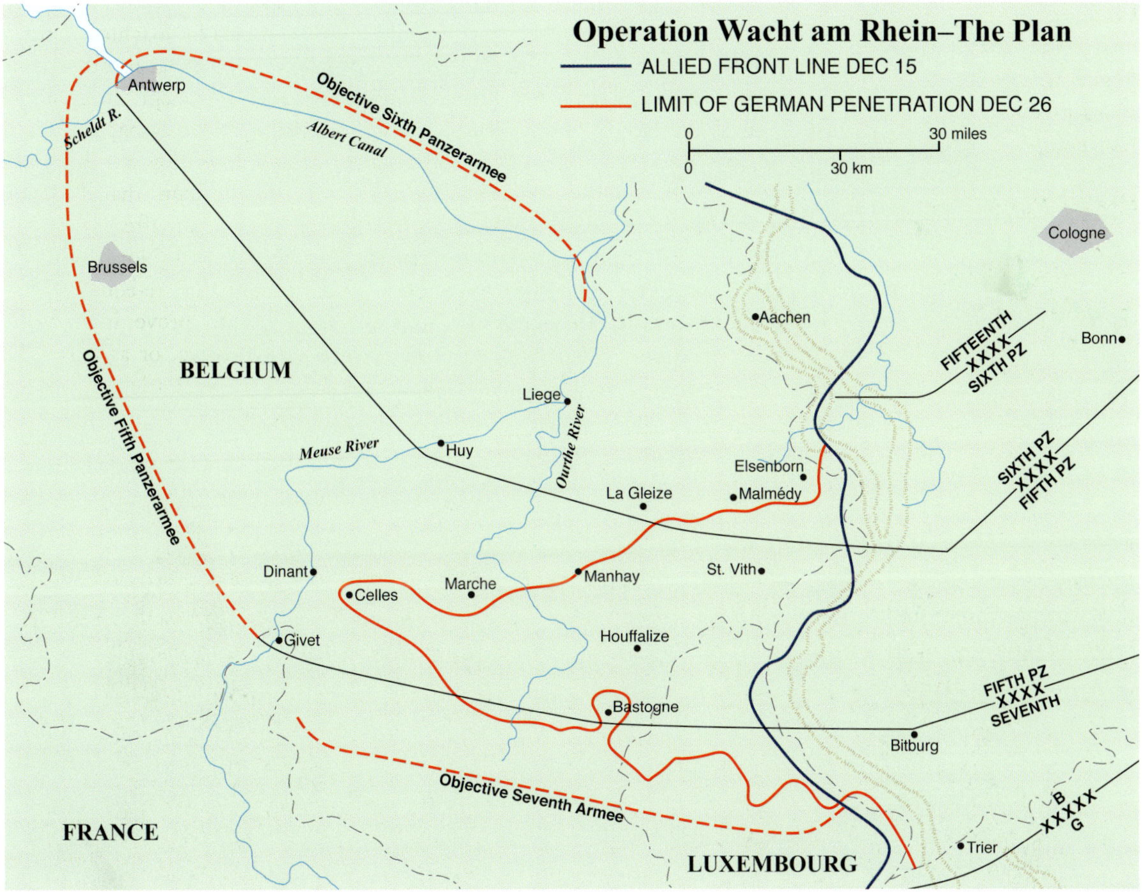

**Right:**
SS-Sturmbannführer Gustav Knittel (1914–76) commanded Schnell Gruppe Knittel, formed around the Leibstandarte's 1st SS-Pz Reconnaissance Battalion.

**Far Right:**
SS-Oberführer Wilhelm Mohnke (1911–2001) commanded LSSAH during the Battle of the Bulge.

**Below:**
The extent of the "Bulge."

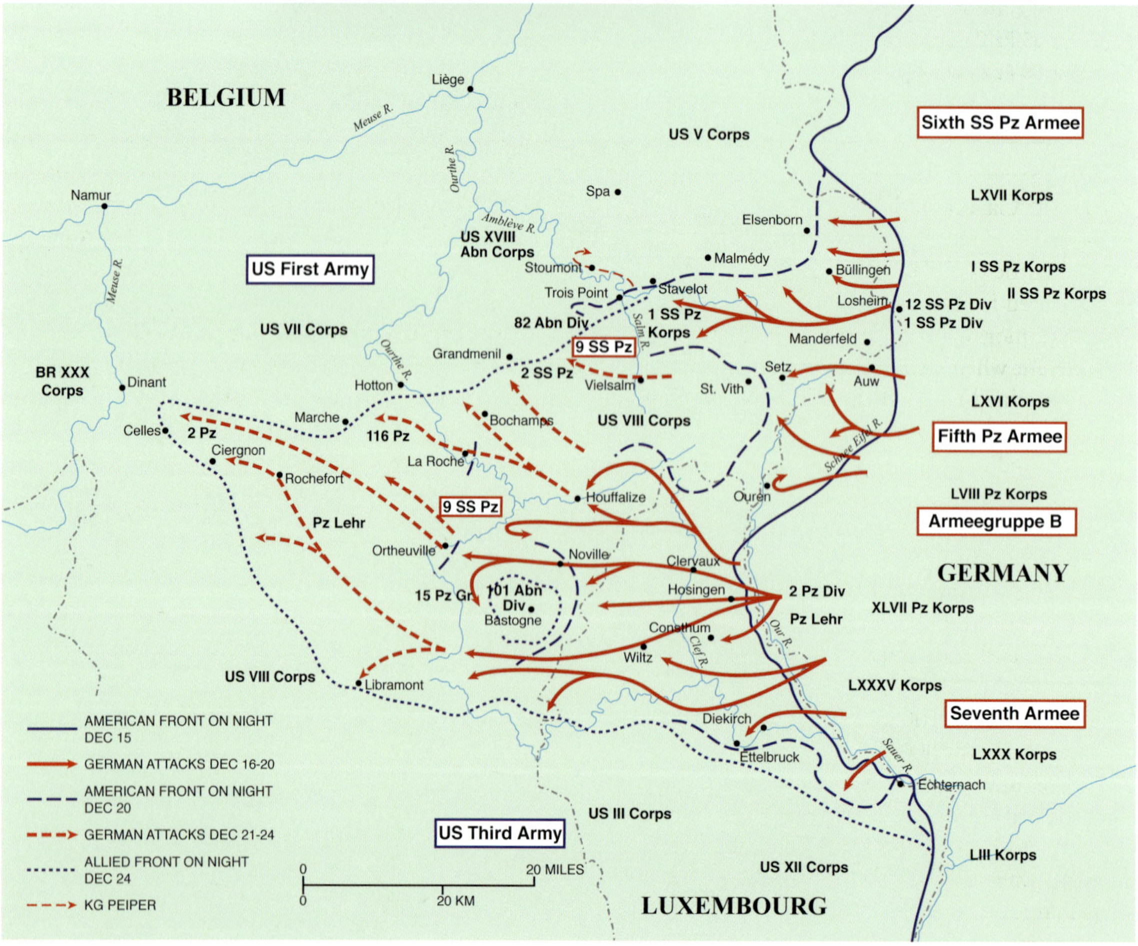

# ORDER OF BATTLE OF LEIBSTANDARTE
## Under the command of: Oberführer Wilhelm Mohnke

**KG Peiper** (SS-Obersturmbannfüher Peiper)
I./1st SS-Pz Regt with 1. and 2. Coys (38 PzKpfw Vs), 6. and 7. Coys (34 PzKpfw IVs), 9. Coy (Engr), 10. Coy (AAA—4 x 37mm; 4 x 20mm; 3 x Wirbelwinds)
501st sSSPzAbt should have had 45 PzKpfw VI Tiger IIs but probably only around 20
III./2nd SS-PzGr Regt SPWs with 3 x Rifle Coys, 1 x Hy Weapons Coy, and 1 x Inf Gun Coy with 6 x 150mm
II./1st SS-Pz Arty Regt with 3 x coys each with 6 x towed 105mm guns
3./1st SS-Pz Engr Bn
84th Luftwaffe Flak Bn with 20mm/37mm AAA guns
SS-Pz Supply Coy and SS-Pz Repair Coy

**Schnell Gruppe Knittel** (Sturmbannführer Gustav Knittel)
1st SS-Pz Reconnaisance Abt
2./1st SS-Pz Engr Bn
II./1st SS-Pz Arty Regt

**KG Sandig** (SS-Standartenfüher Sandig)
2nd SS-PzGr Regt less IIIrd Bn (to KG Peiper)
III./1st SS-Pz Arty Regt
14th SS-Pz AAA Coy
15th SS-Pz Engr Coy

**KG Hansen** (SS-Standartenfüher Hansen)
1st SS-PzGr Regt
1st SS-PzJgr Abt
I./1st SS-Pz Arty Regt—Werfer Bn with 18 x 150mm and 6 x 210mm
13th Inf Gun Coy with 6 x 150mm guns
14th SS-Pz AAA Coy with 12 x 20mm guns
15th SS-Pz Engr Coy
IV./1st SS-Pz Arty Regt with 6 x 105mm guns
I./1st SS-Pz Engr Bn

The division also had a number of units from 150 Panzer Brigade. Peiper said 500 men, 20 M4s, a few German tanks, 30 trucks, and 30–50 jeeps—but these numbers seem unlikely.

## Battle Casualties

The Battle of the Bulge lasted for a full month, as measured from the start of the German offensive on the morning of December 16, 1944, to the moment when elements of First Army and Third Army joined hands at the village of Houffalize on January 16, 1945. Even then the fighting continued as the Germans withdrew, St. Vith only being retaken on the 23rd. By the end the battle had involved some 600,000 American troops, supported by British along the Meuse, and 400,000 Germans.

Casualties are often stated as approximately 80,000 on the Allied side and 100,000 Germans; however, immediate post-battle reports or estimates are not necessarily accurate. A further study from the U.S. Dept. of the Army assessed 108,347 losses on the American side (19,246 dead, 62,489 wounded, 26,612 captured/missing), while the German High Command noted 81,834 total losses for the period December 16–January 26 on the entire Western front.

Kampfgruppe Peiper consisted of 4,800 men and 800 vehicles: 770 men made it back to Wanne on December 25. KG Hansen lost at least 500 men at Stavelot and KG Kittel almost 300.

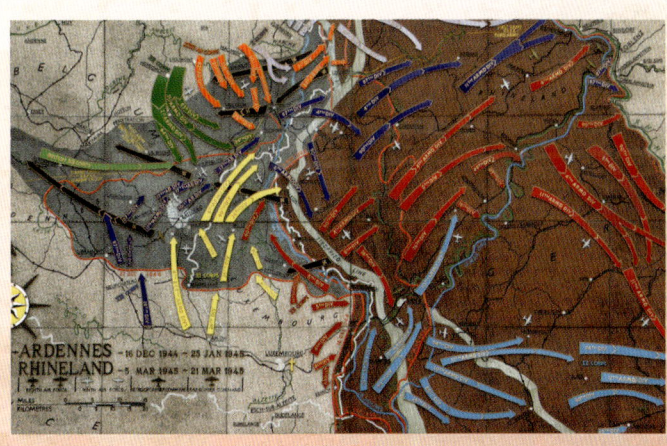

**Above:**
The weather and the road conditions were treacherous. Peiper commented, "these roads were not for tanks, but were for bicycles" ... let alone Tiger IIs.

**Left:**
Allied airpower dominated the battlefield when the skies were clear. The Germans launched Operation Bodenplatte on January 1, 1945, in a vain attempt to wrest the initiative. The Allies lost hundreds of aircraft, mainly on the ground, but they could be replaced quickly. What the Germans could not replace were their 250 pilots killed or taken POW.

**Opposite:**
Many of the King Tigers of 501st sSSPzAbt were lost or abandoned when Peiper escaped from La Gleize.

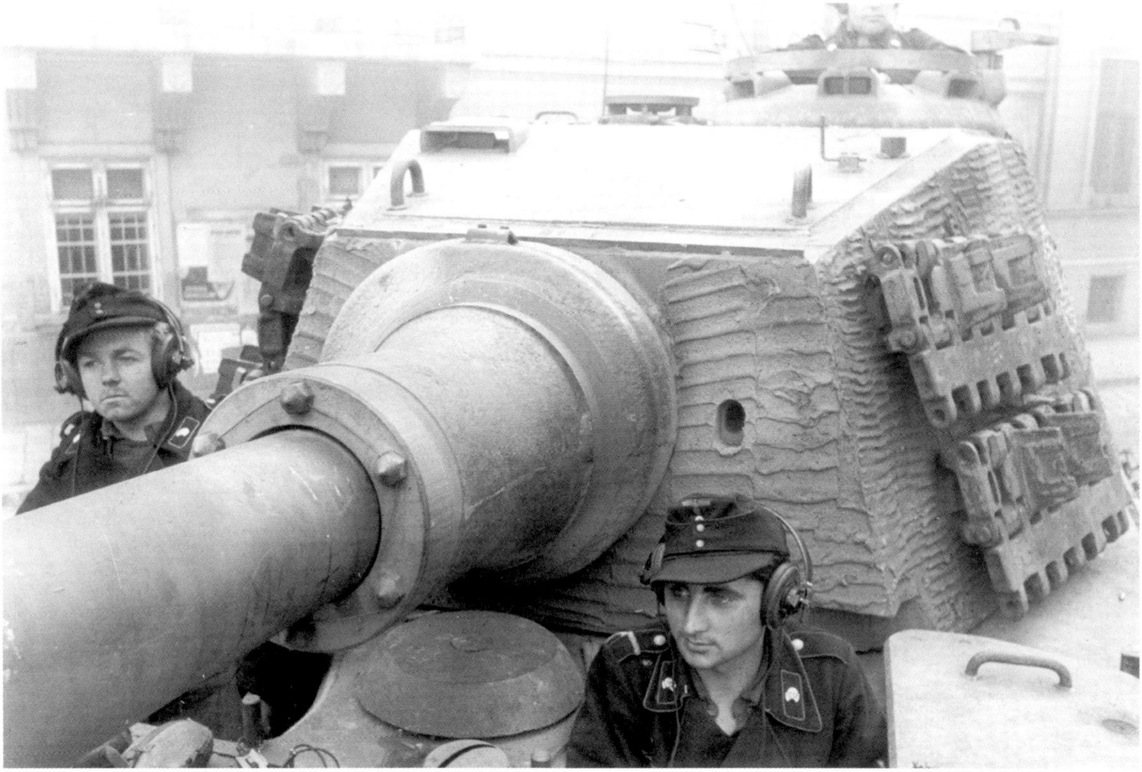

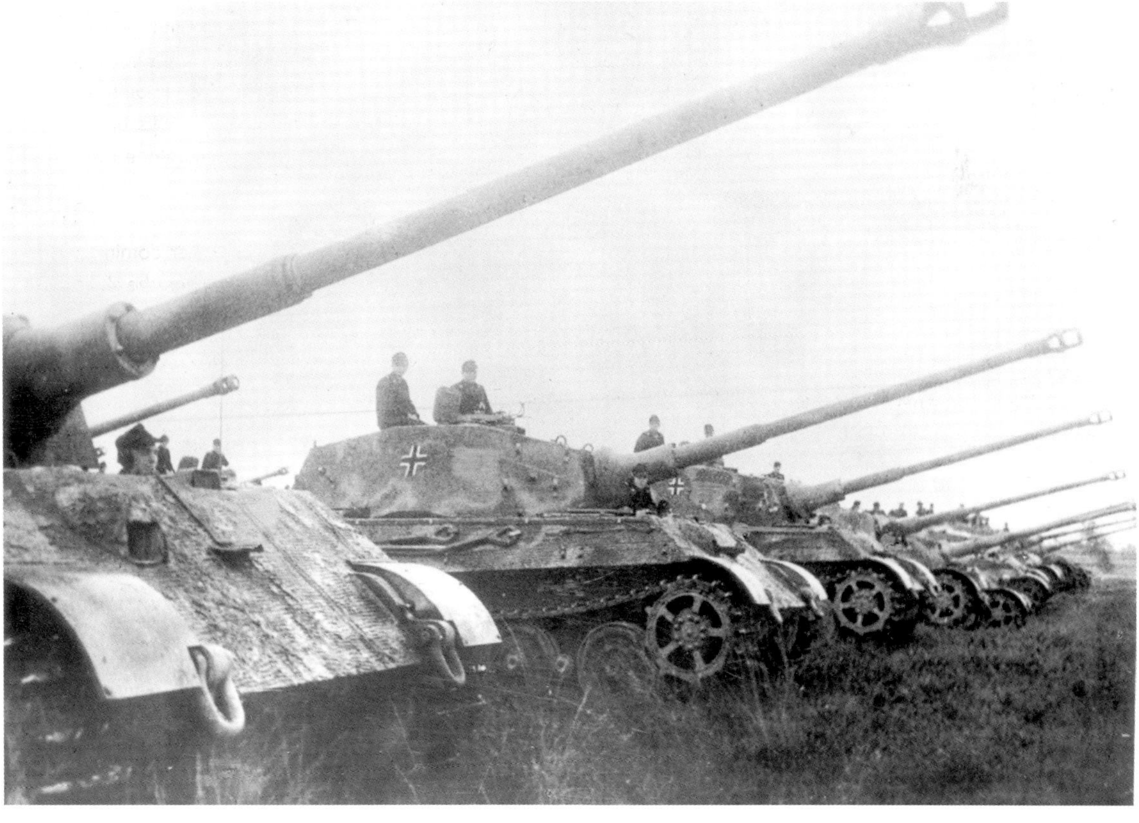

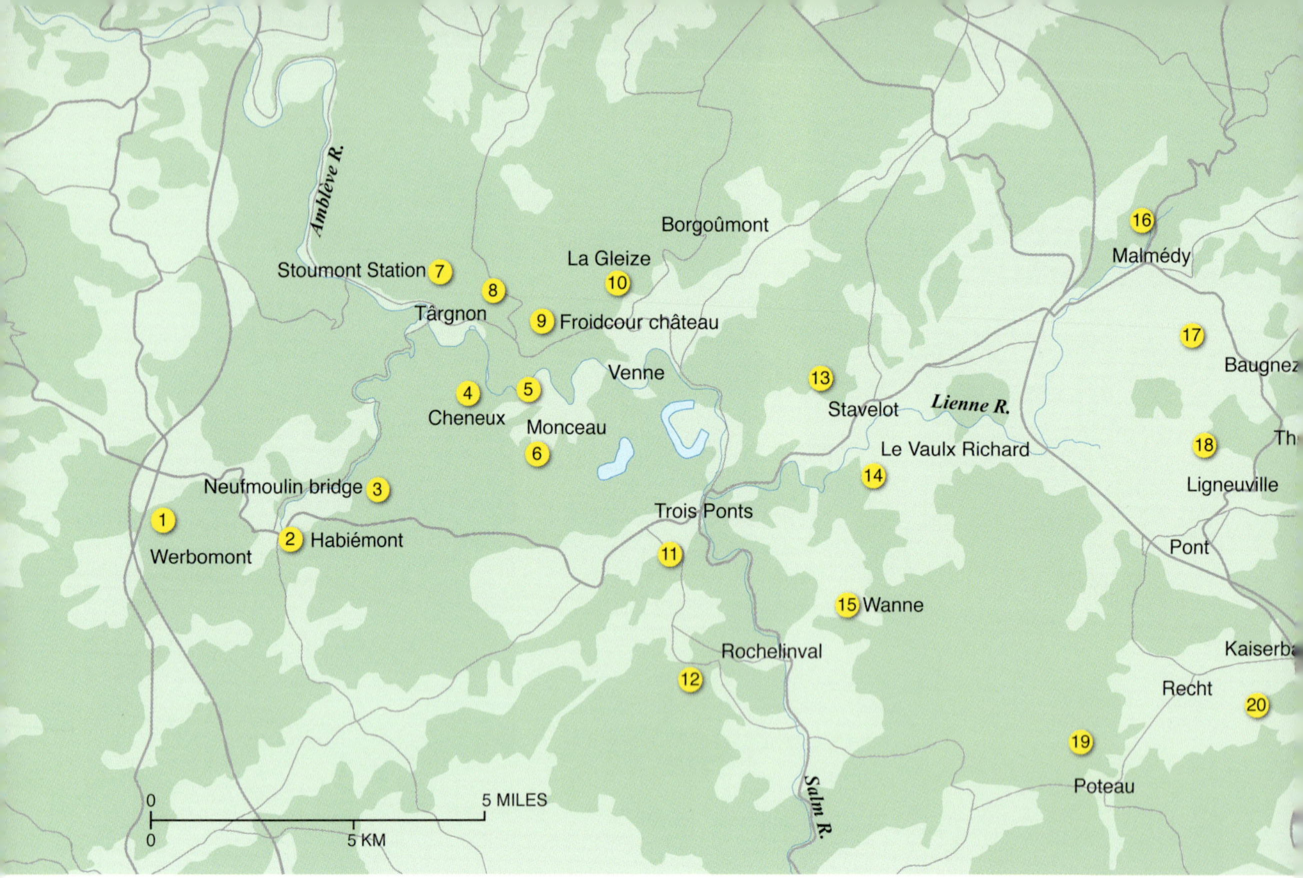
Amblève R.
Borgoûmont
La Gleize
10
Stoumont Station
7
8
Târgnon
9
Froidcour château
Venne
4
5
Cheneux
Monceau
6
Neufmoulin bridge
3
1
Werbomont
2
Habiémont
Trois Ponts
11
Rochelinval
12
13
Stavelot
Lienne R.
Le Vaulx Richard
14
15
Wanne
Salm R.
16
Malmédy
17
18
Ligneuville
Pont
Recht
20
19
Poteau
0
5 MILES
0
5 KM

213

**Above:**
The area today. Museums, memorials, and other visible signs of the battle as detailed in the book.
1 Werbomont 82nd AB memorial.
2 Habiemont commemorative marker.
3 Neufmoulin bridge memorial
4 Cheneux memorial and explanation board
5 Cheneux: Peiper's Pillbox and explanation board
6 Monceau explanation board
7 Stoumont Station marker
8 Târgnon plaque on church
9 Froidcour château
10 La Gleize museum and King Tiger
11 Trois Ponts memorials
12 Rochelinval memorial
13 Stavelot marker, Wall plaques and bridge plaque
14 Chemin de château monument
15 Wanne memorial and château
16 Malmédy memorial to civilian dead
17 Baugnez crossroads memorial and museum
18 Ligneuville memorial
19 Poteau memorial and museum
20 Kaiserbaracke crossroads
21 Wereth 11 memorial
22 Honsfeld memorial
23 Lanzerath memorial
24 Losheim memorial
25 Scheid railway bridge

**Opposite:**
Today, La Gleize is a site of pilgrimage for armor fans as it boasts the only Tiger II visible to the public from the roadside, one of only seven survivors of the 489 built. 213 was disabled while sited near Wérimont Farm, to the south of the village. Armeegruppe B lost 13 Tiger IIs in the Ardennes: including six in La Gleize (see p. 54) and two in Stavelot (see p. 32).

**Right:**
Leibstandarte men were involved in a number of atrocities, from the massacre at Baugnez crossroads (as shown here) to the slaughter of civilians in the Stavelot area.

# LSSAH History

**Below:**
Accompanied by Sepp Dietrich and SS-Sturmbannführer Jürgen Wagner, Hitler inspects the LSSAH on the Berlin Lichterfelde parade ground. A Prussian cadet training school, it was taken over by the LSSAH and a HQ building was constructed.

**Opposite, Above:**
Dietrich leads the LSSAH in Nürnberg during the 1935 Parteitag—Nazi Party congress.

**Opposite, Below:**
Hitler accompanied by staff and bodyguard is cheered by troops during the Polish campaign. Leibstandarte performed well in the campagn, although the army felt SS units took unnecessary risks that accounted for overly heavy losses.

Soon after taking power in 1933, Adolf Hitler instructed his personal bodyguard, Sepp Dietrich, to expand Berlin's existing Chancellory Guard into an elite special unit: the Leibstandarte SS Adolf Hitler. Originally consisting of 117 carefully chosen men, by the time World War II began the largely ceremonial unit had been expanded into a full combat regiment. This was still the period, however, when a physical flaw as minor as a tooth cavity could disqualify one from the unit. Those standards would certainly relax as the war continued.

Having proven its combat value in Poland, the Leibstandarte would continue to be upgraded and expanded after nearly every campaign. By 1940 in France it was a motorized regiment, in the Balkans it was the size of a brigade, and by the invasion of Russia it was a small division of 10,000 men. Thereafter it would be converted into a large panzergrenadier division, and by the time of the Allies' Normandy invasion it was a full panzer division.

The other side of the coin was that, as a cutting edge of German combat power, the Leibstandarte continually had to be rebuilt as it suffered horrific losses. It emerged from the first winter in Russia as a frozen skeleton of a unit, and was further decimated in 1943 by Manstein's Kharkov counteroffensive and the Battle of Kursk. More losses were incurred in 1943 when the LSSAH had to hand over a number of officers and cadre to help form the SS Hitlerjugend (Hitler Youth) Division—the 12th SS.

In Normandy the Leibstandarte again suffered grievous casualties by the time it squeezed out of the Falaise Pocket. However, once more it was quickly rebuilt, until by December 1944 it was a very large division of some 19,500 men with 3,000 vehicles. While many of the new recruits were young, inexperienced, and barely trained, it seemed that nearly all of them were imbued—for better or worse—with the *ésprit d'corps* that came from belonging to the premier division of the Waffen SS.

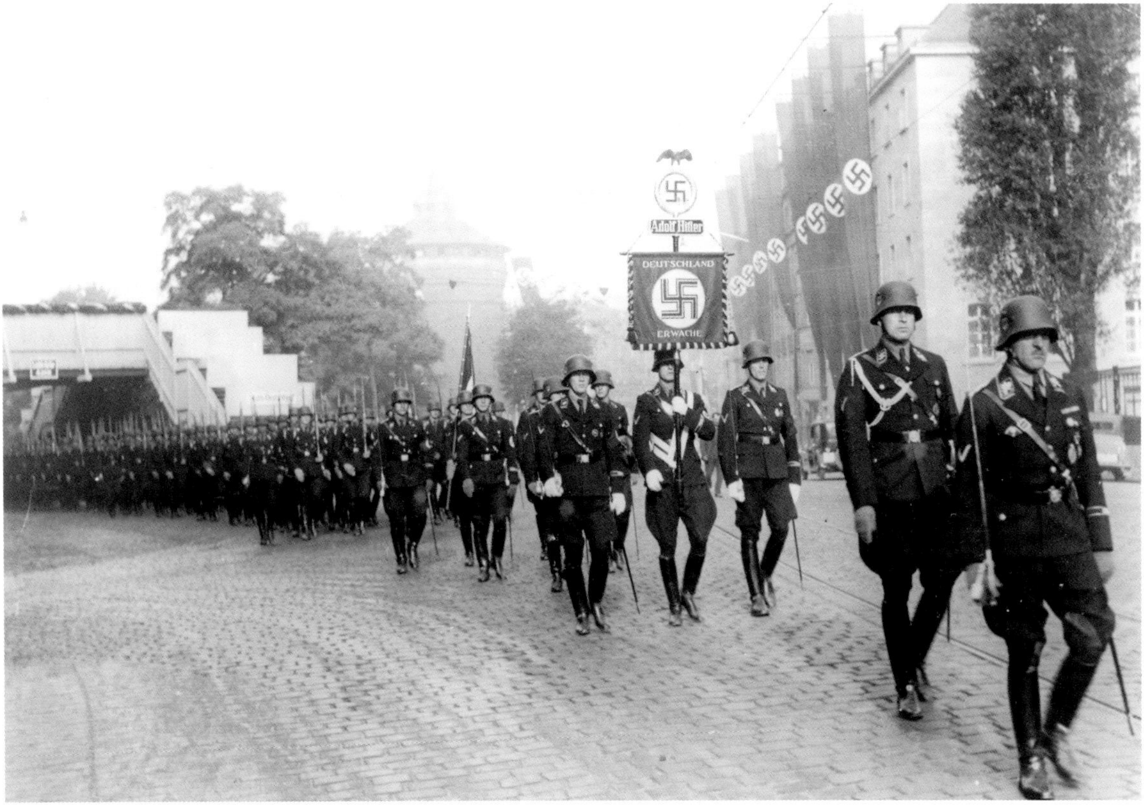
Adolf Hitler
DEUTSCHLAND
ERWACHE

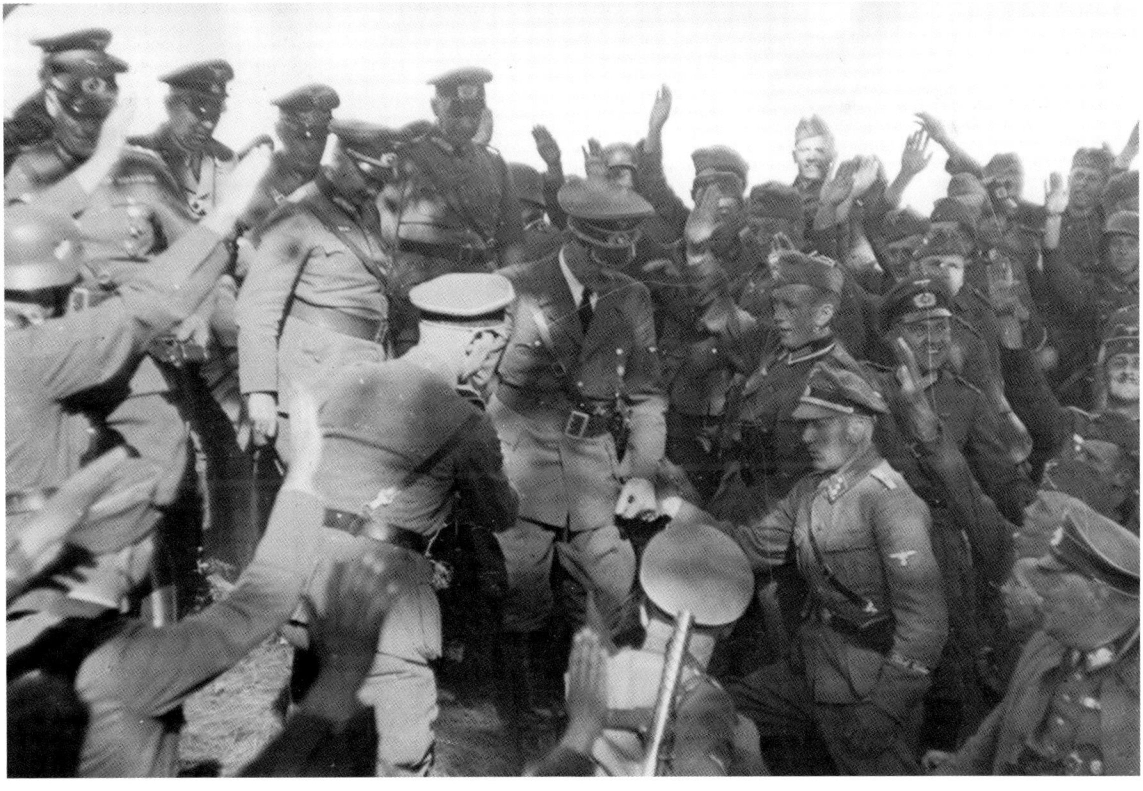

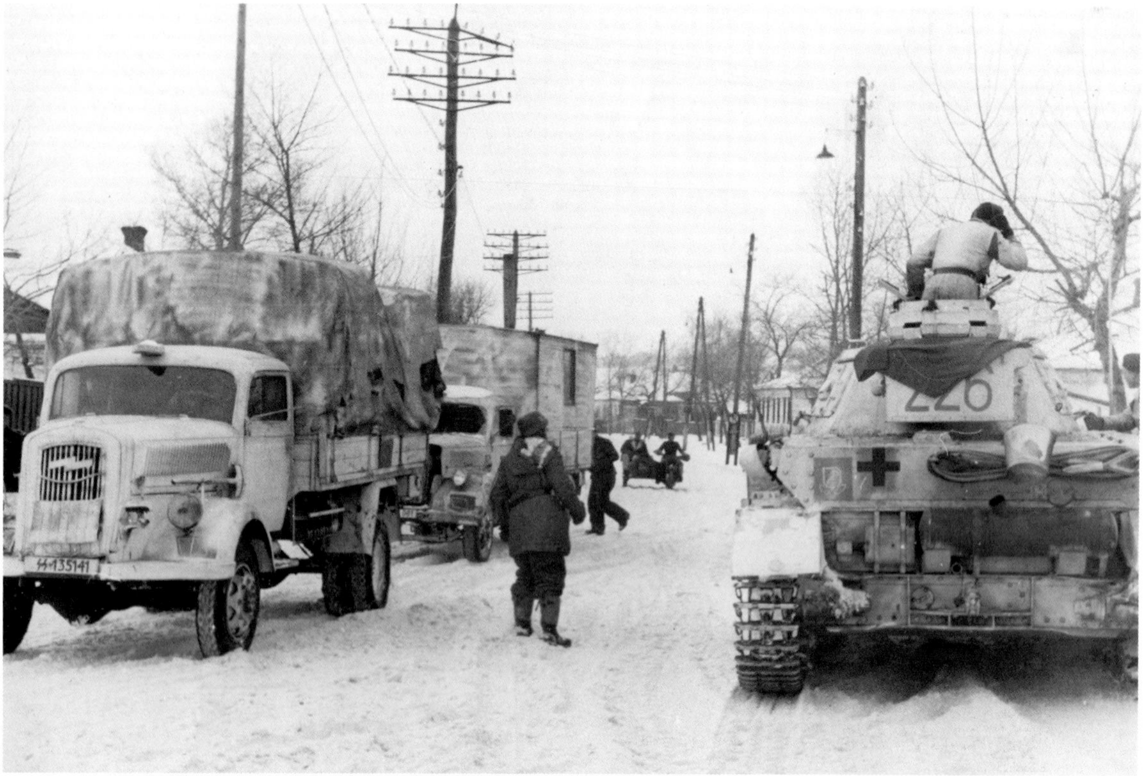
226

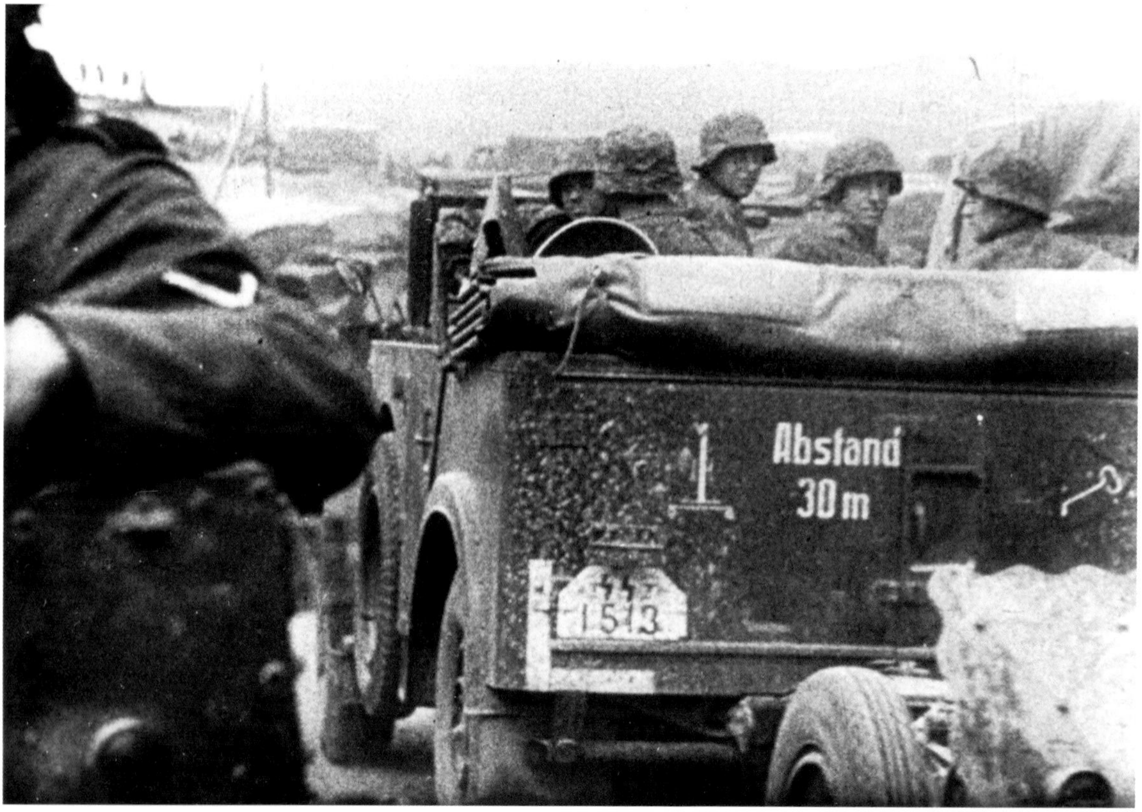
Abstand
30 m
1513

**Opposite, Above:**
LSSAH in Russia. By now an armored division in all but name, Leibstandarte gained a reputation for both its fighting ability and its brutality. Hundreds of Russian civilians were killed in retaliation and reprisals for injuries to their own troops.

**Opposite, Below:**
The skeleton key insignia and instruction to leave 30m between vehicles was typical of LSSAH.

**Above:**
The end of the Normandy campaign. An M4 and a PzKpfw IV from LSSAH's 7./1st SS-Pz Regt on the Falaise–Argentan road, between the towns of Saint-Lambert-sur-Dive and Chambois, August 1944.

**Left:**
LSSAH cuff title inspected by British VIII Corps (note the knight on horseback cloth badge) staff officers.

15

# The Plan

**Below:** SS Oberstgruppenführer Sepp Dietrich (1892–1966) commanded Sixth Panzer Army in the Ardennes. While some say he was promoted beyond his capabilities, Dietrich was an immensely capable front-line commander who had the respect of his troops. Unlike many other senior officers he was also prepared to argue with Hitler, particularly his no retreat policy. Dietrich was found guilty of complicity in the Malmédy massacre and spent some years in prison. When released in 1955, he was prosecuted and jailed for his part in the 1934 "Night of the Long Knives."

Hitler's aims for the Ardennes Offensive were grandiose, as always. He intended for the Sixth SS Panzer Army, supported by Fifth Panzer Army, to bounce the Meuse River, overrun the great Allied supply center at Liege, and drive on toward the port of Antwerp, thus severing from behind all of Montgomery's 21st Army Group plus half of US First Army—30 Allied divisions in all.

Most of Hitler's senior generals, from Gerd von Rundstedt to Walther Model, naturally thought this was nonsense—at least beyond Germany's reach at this point in the war. However, they did see promise in the plan if they could execute what they termed "the small solution" (as opposed to Hitler's fantasy)—cutting behind the US concentration at Aachen and the Roer River, and otherwise create havoc among the US supply net. They could put the Western Allies back on their heels, relaxing pressure on the rest of the front, thence be able to concentrate anew on their more forbidding adversary in the East. And who knew? If a surprise counteroffensive could trap and destroy a number of American divisions, it might have a cascading psychological effect on the entire Allied effort.

Sepp Dietrich's Sixth SS Panzer Army would lead the offensive, spearheaded by Ist SS-Panzer Corps, headed by the 1st SS Division—Leibstandarte SS Adolf Hitler—and its younger sibling, the 12th SS Hitlerjugend. The army planned five exact routes for the advance, north to south, listed A to E. Hitlerjugend would adhere to A, B, C, while the Leibstandarte would have routes D and E. Any derivation from these routes was strictly forbidden—no unit could go freelancing, thus jeopardize the essential target of the Meuse.

Infantry units were designated to attack first, thus open the way for the panzer divisions. As the date of the offensive approached, Hermann Priess, commander of Ist SS Panzer Corps, submitted two requests: first, that he be allowed to shift his sector farther south where there were better roads; second, that he be allowed to use his armor for the initial breakthrough. Both requests were refused. As it turned out, the Leibstandarte did achieve a breakthrough; it was the congestion on the roads behind that doomed it.

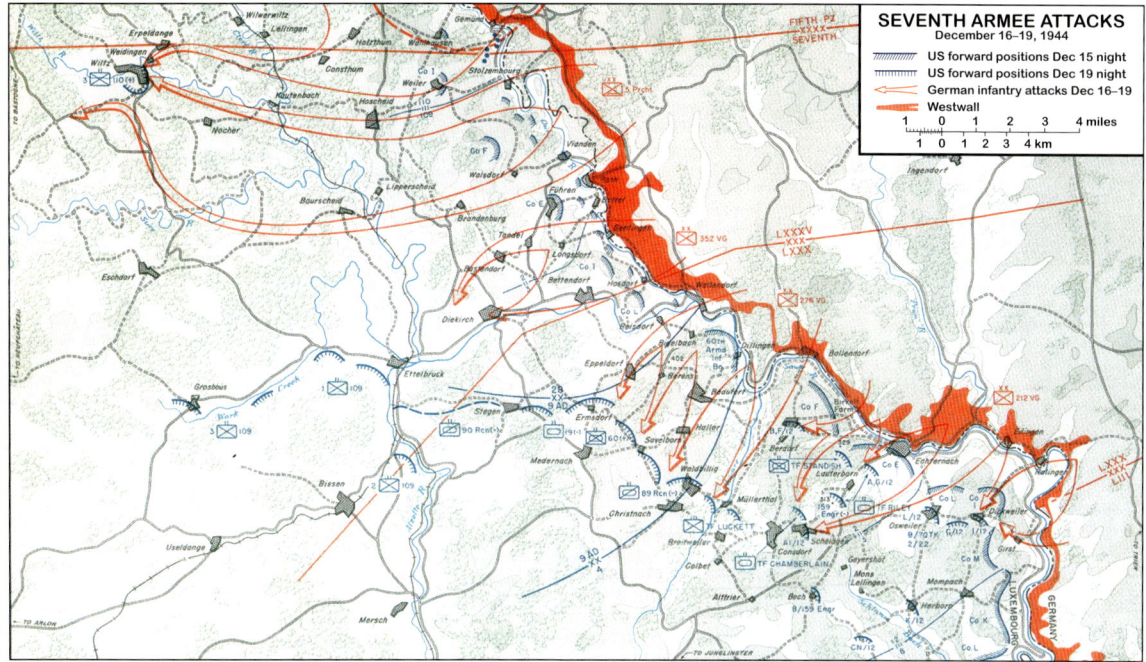

**Above:**
The crucial northern shoulder saw Hitlerjugend held on Elsenborn Ridge by the US 1st Inf Div and Leibstandarte in the valleys to the west by 30th Inf and 82nd Airborne.

**Below:**
The Rollbahns gave Hitlerjugend the three northerly and Leibstandarte the two southerly tracks: Rollbahn D shared by KG Peiper, first, and KG Sandig. KG Hansen was first on Rollbahn E, followed by KG Knittel. Peiper said in a postwar briefing: "I decided that my column would be about 25km long, and the vehicles would proceed at medium speed. It was impossible for the vehicles in the rear to overtake those in the front because of the bad roads. Therefore, all combat elements had to be placed in the front of the column ..."

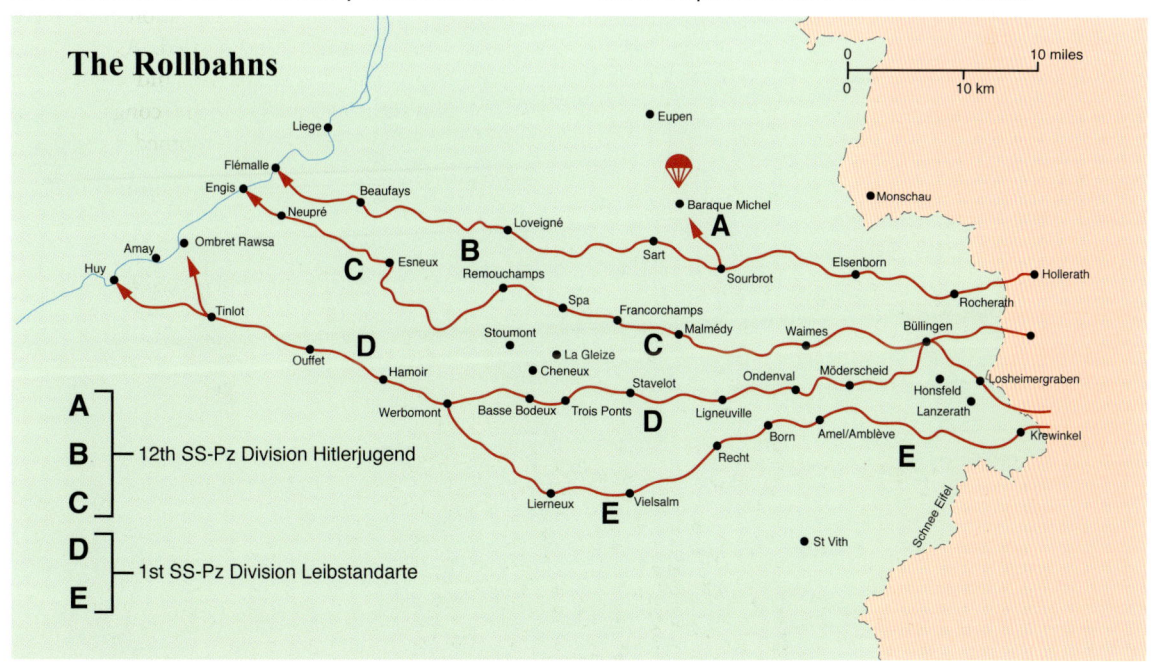

# Into Action

**Opposite, Above:**
A Panther of 12th SS-Pz Div Hitlerjugend burns near Krinkelt. The tenacious US defense cost the division heavily—nearly 10,000 men, including over 300 officers and some 1,700 NCOs.

**Opposite, Below:**
The German timetable was put out of kilter by the staunch American defense.

**Below:**
Memorial to 99th Inf Div's I&R Platoon at Lanzerath.

The great German offensive began precisely as scheduled on Sixth SS Panzer Army's front—announced by the thunderous salvo of 1,000 guns. However, the first day's attacks by the 12th Volksgrenadier and 3rd Fallschirmjäger divisions didn't make nearly the progress expected, knocking the timetable akilter from the start.

German infantry encountered surprisingly dogged resistance from the US 99th Infantry Division, and by mid-afternoon a path for the panzers had not been cleared. Although the US 99th has invariably been called a "green" division, it was activated in 1942 and its men had trained for two years before finally getting to the ETO. They were not going to disgrace themselves now, especially when facing Wehrmacht units just formed in the past few months.

At the village of Lanzerath, an I&R platoon of the US 99th showed its mettle. All afternoon some 20 men held on against repeated attacks from Fallschirmjäger. Finally they ran out of ammo and surrendered, one dead and 14 others wounded. But they had inflicted some 50–70 casualties on their assailants.

Back in the LSSAH column, Peiper grew increasingly frustrated at the delay, so just bulled his armored column through the roads and reached Lanzerath by 11:00 at night. There he was astonished to see the German paratroopers and everyone else asleep. After fierce words with the commander he hijacked a battalion of Fallschirmjäger to accompany his own spearhead. Some of them he spread out to the woods on either side; others rode atop the decks of Tiger II tanks.

By 03:30 Peiper's column was on the move, mopping up isolated US units on the way. It was still dark when they reached the village of Honsfeld, and though a Panther was disabled by bazooka-fire on its outskirts, when the Germans broke in they were surprised to see US military vehicles parked on all the streets, and most of the soldiers asleep in the houses.

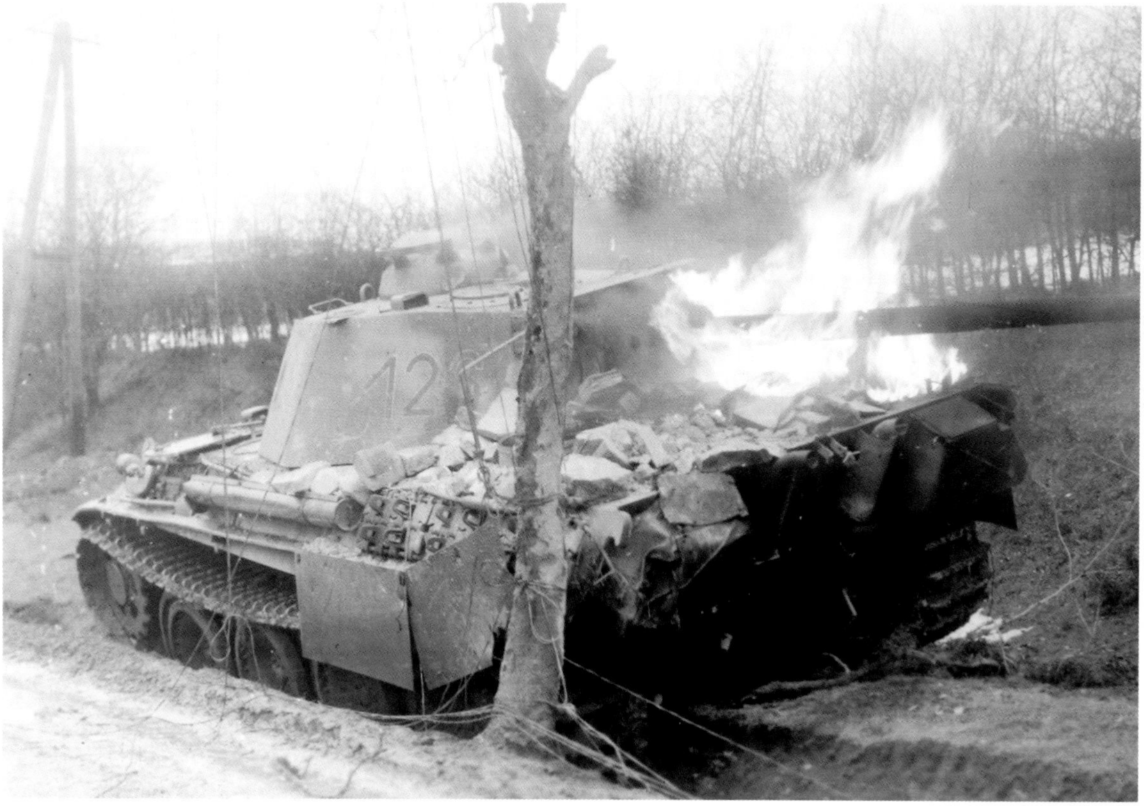

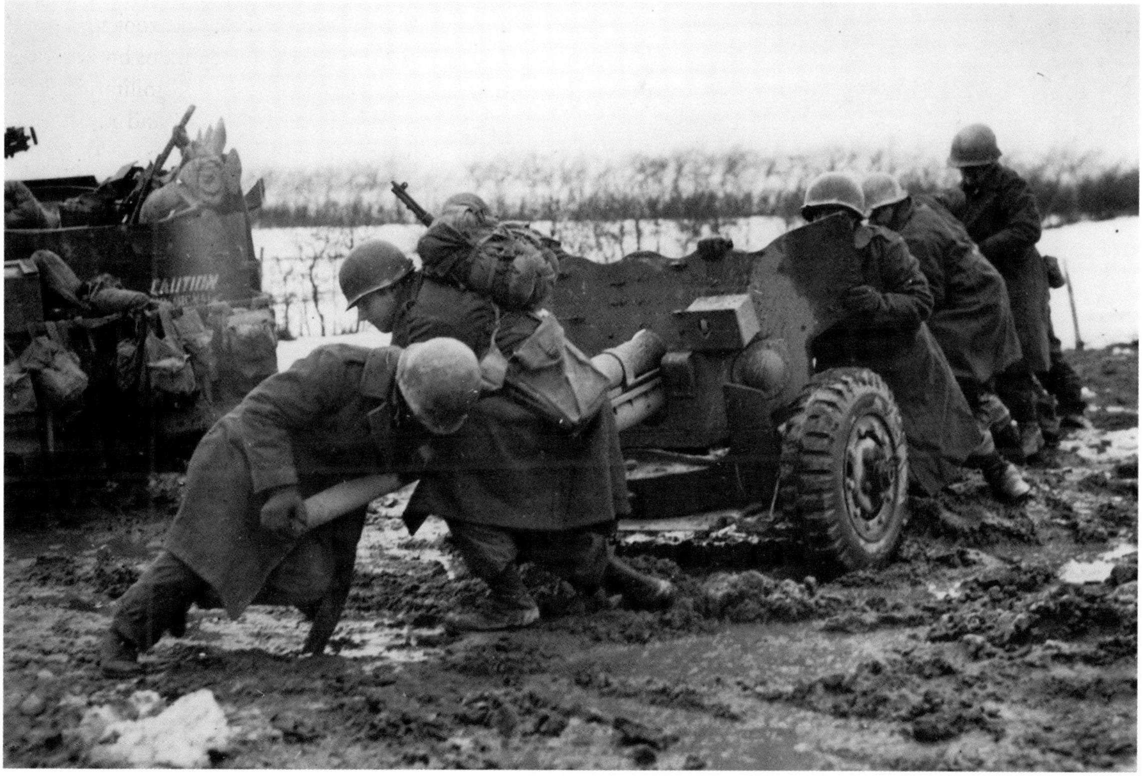

**Below**
Scheid railway bridge over the Malmédy–Stadtkyll railway line had been blown during the German retreat. Today, the line is a cycle path. Peiper's armored column crossed the tracks here at around 14:00 on the 16th.

**Opposite, Above and Below**
The replacement bridge was in place around 16:00 allowing trucks and other vehicles to make their way acoss the border. Note the Flak 38 20mm gun providing AA defense.

German infantry quickly rounded up about 300 prisoners and were taking inventory of their captured booty when firing suddenly erupted from the north part of town. Some Americans were still resisting, firing from windows, and the Germans had to root them out. Calm was restored again when suddenly two more Panthers went up in flames, the work of more US hold-outs.

For this reason or some other, SS men became furious and began to shoot many of their US prisoners. At least 19 were killed in cold blood while the rest were sent off to the rear.

Peiper himself had decided to divert his column on to Büllingen, a village designated as part of Hitlerjugend's route. But he could tell the HJ was still stalled at the frontier, plus he had heard of a US fuel dump there. Büllingen—as a support base for both the 99th and 2nd US infantry divisions—was only occupied by rear-area units, and some 200 more Americans were taken prisoner. The SS also overran two airfields, filled with L-5 spotter planes. The 99th Div ones had been warned so 11 out of 12 were able to take off in the face of the panzers. The 2nd Div ones were still asleep so 11 out of 12 of those were destroyed. The atrocities at Honsfeld were not repeated at Büllingen—rumors that 50 US POWs who helped to refuel Peiper's panzers were afterward killed proved unfounded.

It is at this juncture that the first of the great "what-if's" about Peiper's drive occurs. If he had headed a mile or so further north to Wirzfeld he could've overrun the HQ of the US 2nd Division, and opened the way for the Hitlerjugend by cutting behind both the 99th and 2nd divisions. At that point, just to Peiper's right, was an estate called Domaine Bütgenbach (the Americans called it "Dom B") at which only a medical station stood.

Instead, after refueling, Peiper got back on his own route D toward the Meuse. After he left, a regiment of the US 1st Infantry Division arrived at Dom B and would continue to hold up the HJ.

*continued on p. 29*

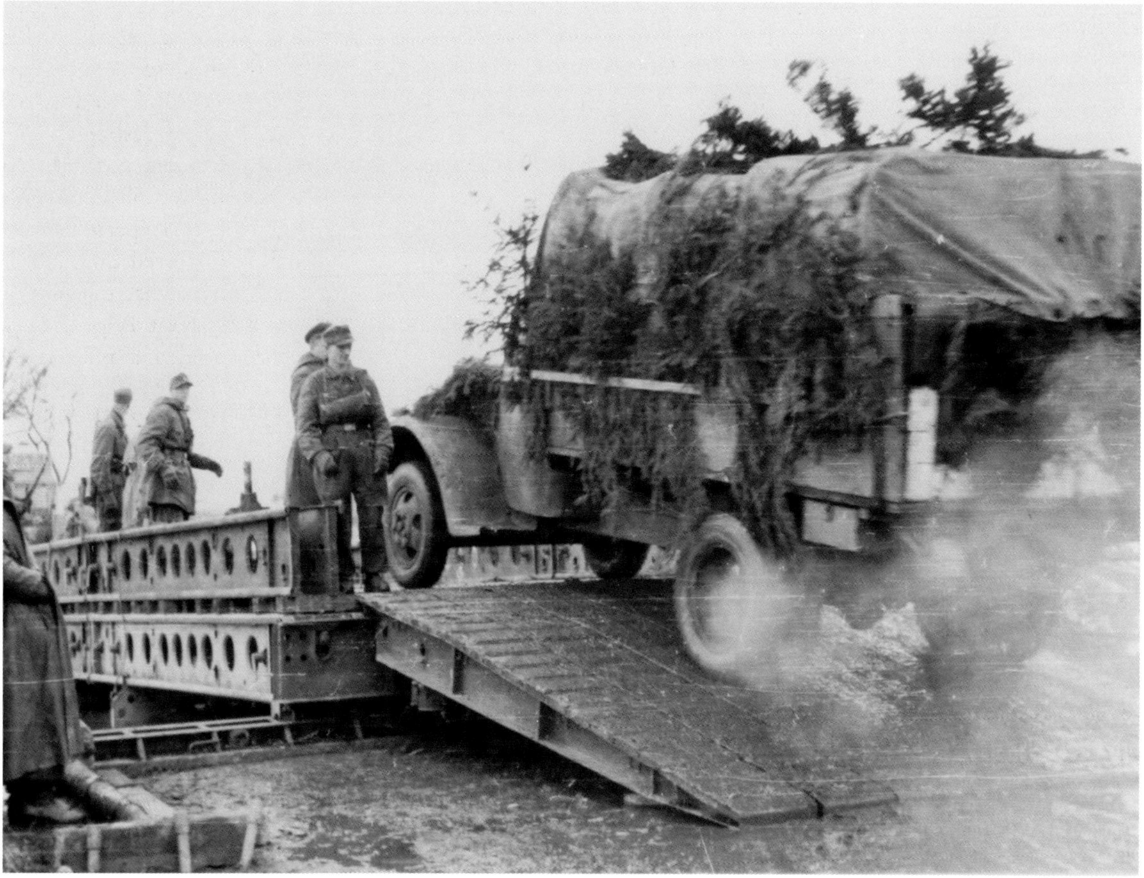

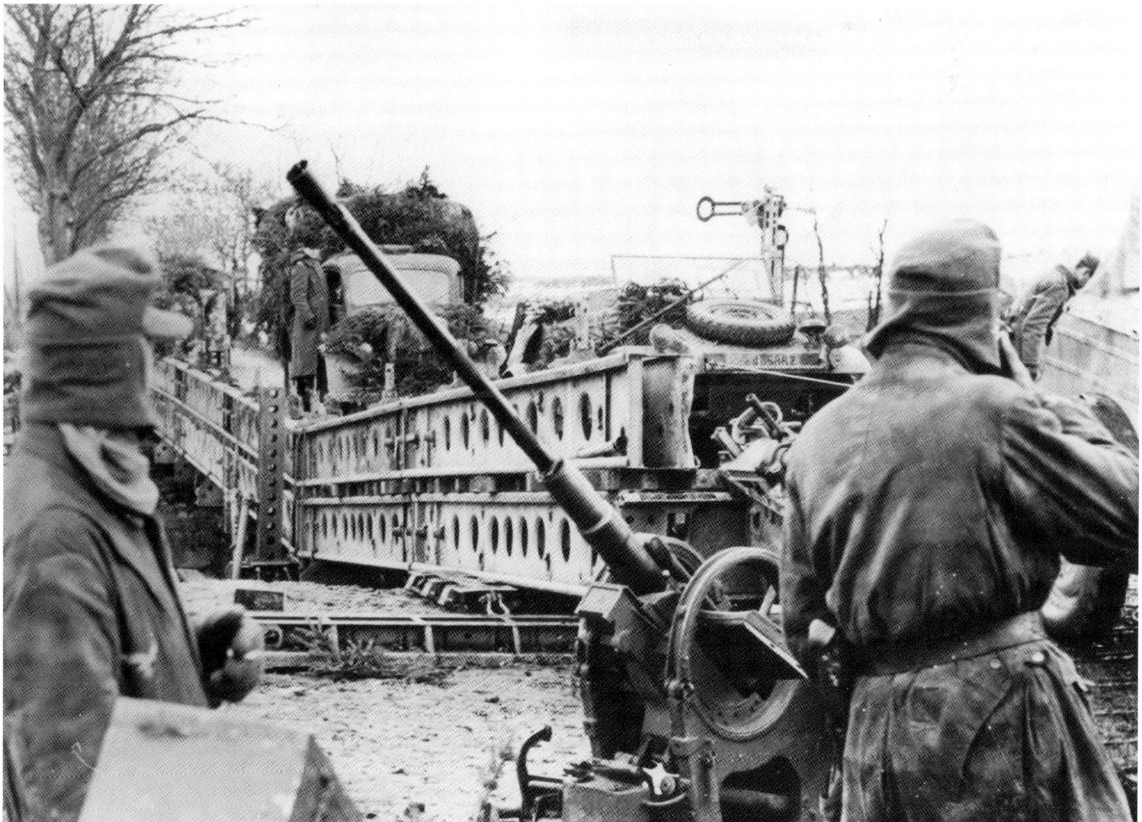

**Above, Left and Right, and Below:**
As one drives along the narrow roads past Merlscheid church, it's easy to envisage the length of the Leibstandarte column—and the easy pickings for US fighter-bombers when they got airborne.

**Opposite, Above and Below:**
Opposite the church this M5 3-inch ATk gun speaks of another holdup to the Leibstandarte advance. Today the farmhouse has seen additions.

# Dec 17

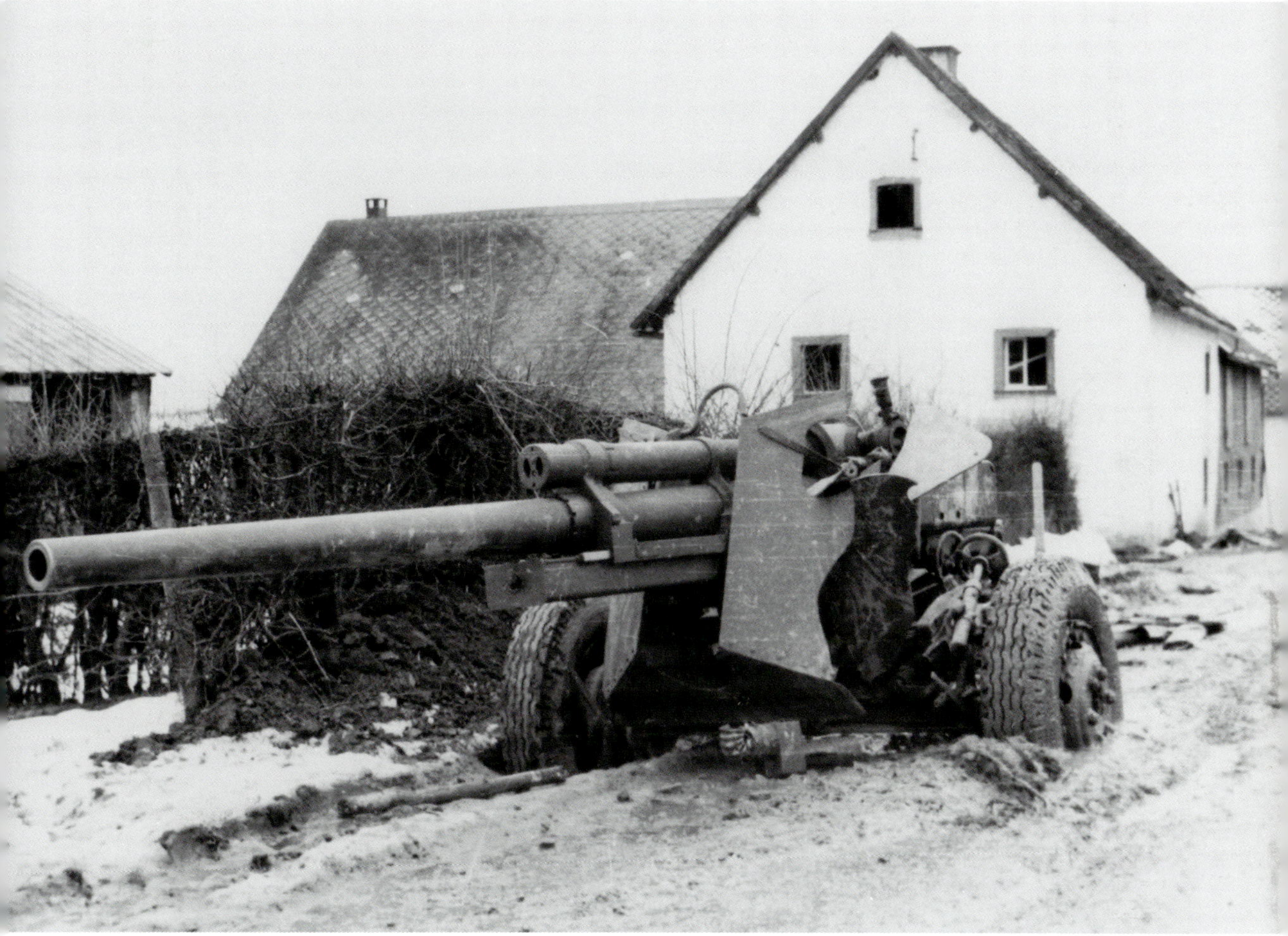

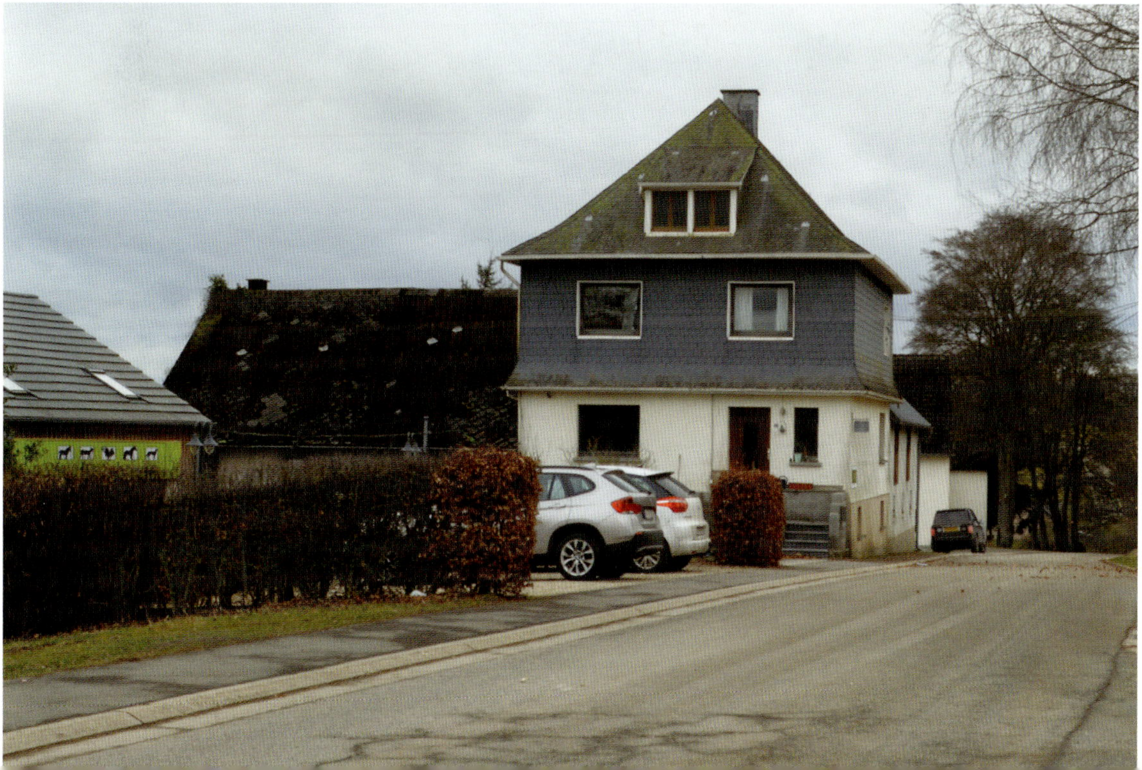

**Above and Inset:** 99th Inf Div POWs make their way through Merlscheid.

**Left:** A King Tiger of 501st sSSPzAbt passes the same POWs as it motors towards Lanzerath.

**Above:**
Another US tank destroyer team has paid the ultimate price. This one was in Honsfeld, probably from 801st TD Bn. The 612th TD Bn had arrived in the village on the 16th but had been sent to rest and not yet deployed their guns.

**Below:**
An SdKfz 251 moves through Honsfeld towards Büllingen. The village was an R&R area for 99th Inf Div—Marlene Dietrich was expected to perform here on December 17 after having played Diekirch on the 16th—and many were asleep when Leibstandarte arrived at 06:00 on the 17th. Not all the captives joined the lines of POWs. As elsewhere, a number were murdered in cold blood. Infiltration of Honsfeld saw units of Operation Greif involved. The *After Action Report of 801st TD Bn* mentions a number of incidents including: "At 0400A the 2nd plat of Co A with three 3" guns reported to its Co Hqs that one American light tank with German occupants had slipped by its gun position and a bazooka team consisting of the plat leader and two men were trying to intercept the tank and destroy it. As the bazooka team moved down the road they noted a convoy of German tanks and vehicles had joined up with the American light tank and all were heading in the direction of HONSFELD. It was also noted that the Germans on the light tank were speaking English."

**Above Left and Left:**
This well-known photo shows Luftwaffe troops changing footwear at the crossroads in Honsfeld on the way to Büllingen. Today, there's a memorial to the 612th and 801st TD Bns attached to 99th Inf Div.

**Above and Below:**
Vehicles parked in a farmyard close to the crossroads. 3rd FJR Div had made the initial breakthrough south of Losheim and one of its units—I./FJR 9—was subordinated to LSSAH. Some of its men, carried by King Tiger 222, will be seen in various photos through the book.

# Malmédy

**Above:**
The Baugnez crossroads today. At **A** (and **Opposite, Center**) the memorial. At **B** the massacre field. At **C** one of the 27 battlefield markers that show the limits of the German advance.

**Below:**
Peiper in captivity.

**Below: Rght**
Men of Bty B, 285th Fd Arty Obs Bn, lie dead in the snow.

**Opposite Top:**
The memorial to the Wereth 11, artillerymen of the 333rd FA Bn, tortured and murdered by men of LSSAH's Kampfgruppe Knittel. The memorial was originally erected by Herman Langer, the son of the farmer, who had given the men food and shelter in the corner of the pasture where they were murdered.

**Opposite Below:**
Sgt. Howard J. Brodie, a staff artist at *Yank* magazine, drew this emotive sketch after talking to survivors.

In obedience to his original orders, Peiper inadvertently left himself without support from his sister division in Ist SS-Panzer Corps.

Continuing to drive west, KG Peiper found itself faced with some farm roads that bogged down the vehicles. So at midday Peiper decided to divert again to the north, this time toward Malmédy, where he could find a paved road again. At Baugnez Crossroads, some three miles short of that town, he encountered a follow-up unit of the US 7th Armored Division.

As is now writ large in history, Peiper's spearhead encountered a US convoy—Battery B of the 285th Artillery Observation Battalion—of some 30 vehicles and 140 men. The SS shot up the convoy, forcing the men to hide in ditches. Peiper was nearby and approved of the order to cease firing and just herd the prisoners off to the side. He and the column's spearhead headed off to Ligneuville, where an American headquarters was reputed to be. Little did he know what his following Kampfgruppe would do to those prisoners. When the rest of KG Peiper came up the road a massacre took place, more than half the prisoners shot in cold blood.

When Peiper pulled into Ligneuville, a US repair depot, plus the HQ of the 149th AA Brigade, there was a brief fight until all the US vehicles were knocked

*continued on p. 32*

29

**Above:**
"We captured 200,000 liters in Büllingen and used fifty American prisoners to fill all of our tanks. This was a lucky break, because by the time we had reached Losheim, we had used up as much gasoline in 25 kilometers as we would normally have used in covering 50 kilometers, on account of the mountainous terrain in the Eifel," Peiper said postwar. "... this was a clean breakthrough, and we continued with very little opposition." Büllingen market square was where the fuel dump was. After the war it was planted and now sports a children's play area.

**Below:**
Ligneuville. This was the hotel that Brig-Gen. Edward W. Timberlake of the 49th AAA Bde vacated just in time, leaving his breakfast on the table for Peiper to enjoy. Mohnke moved his forward CP here. The memorial at **A** is shown in detail on p.61. It remembers the murder of eight prisoners of the 9th Armored Division shot near the Hotel du Moulin by the LSSAH advance guard.

**Opposite, Above and Below:**
After the battle US Ninth Air Force liaison officers tried to claim this Panther as one of their kills. It was, in fact, KO'd in Ligneuville by a Sherman dozer.

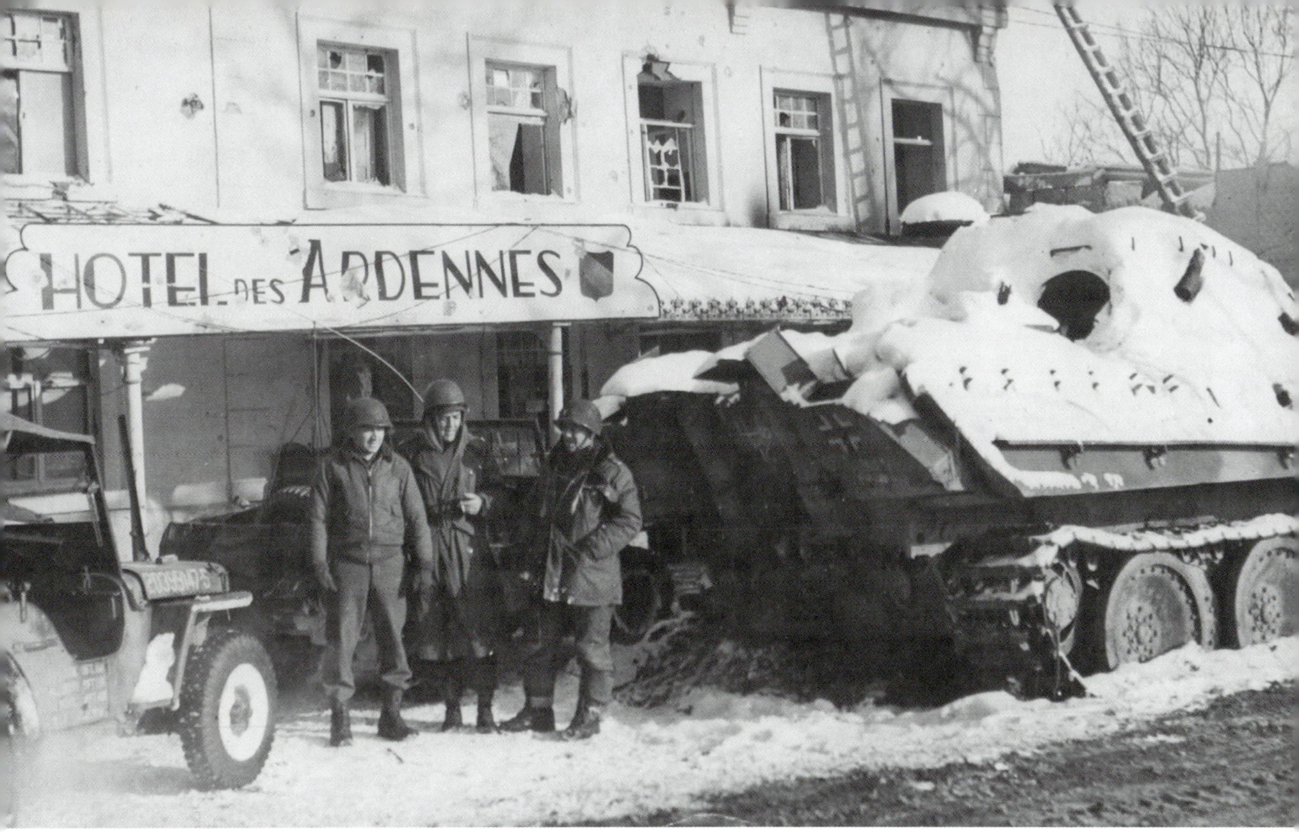
HOTEL DES ARDENNES

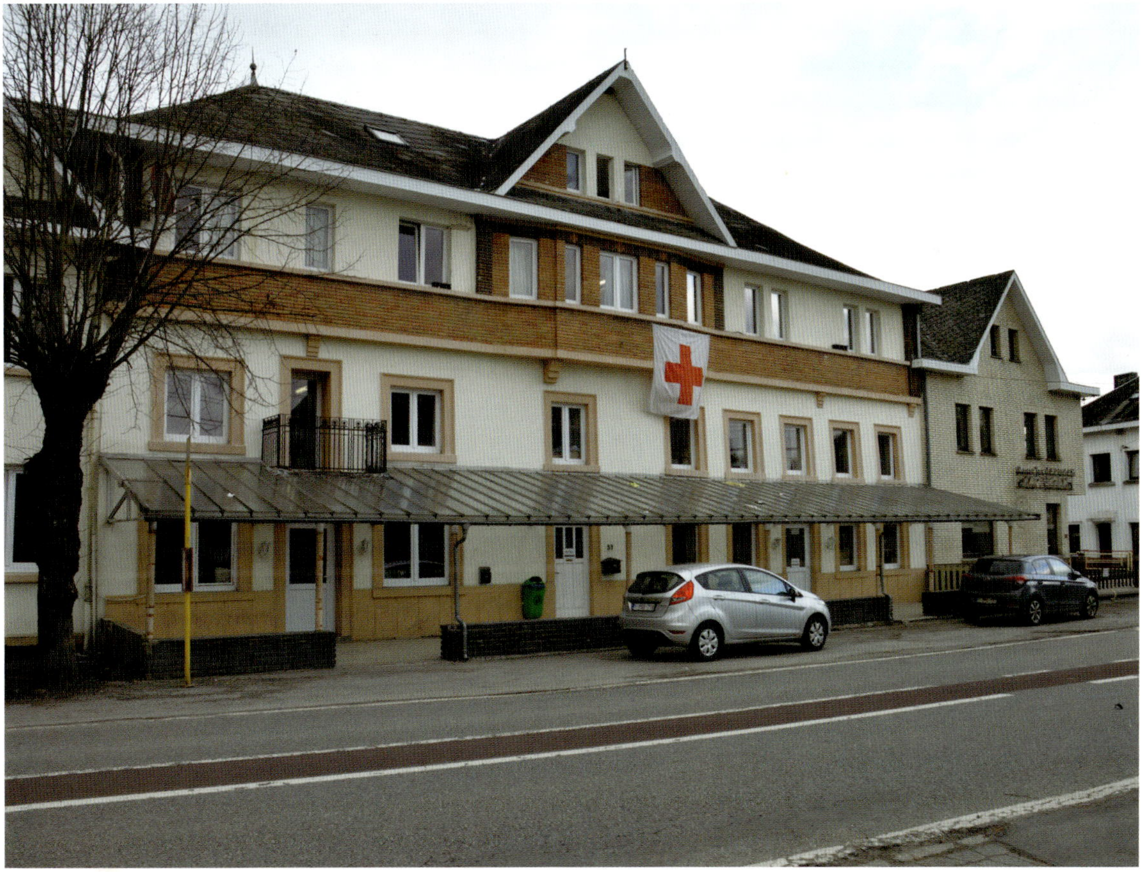

out. Here another atrocity took place as a renegade SS sergeant shot eight US prisoners in the backyard of the Hotel Moulin. The Belgian innkeeper himself, Peter Rupp, witnessed it, and was determined to protect the other 14 US captives on his premises. At first it was a struggle until an SS officer arrived and ordered respect for prisoners. Rupp afterward brought up bottles of cognac to lull the passion of the aggressors.

As the momentous day of December 17 closed, Peiper took a stab toward the bridge over the Amblève River at Stavelot. In the dark, a mere squad of US engineers south of the bridge disabled a Panther with a lucky bazooka-shot. The town itself was full of US vehicles, headlights on, and it was assumed the bridge had been wired for demolition.

Peiper decided to wait for daylight before launching a full assault. He didn't realize that the all the US vehicles in Stavelot that night were either fleeing or heading elsewhere. Besides, his men needed rest, and he was anxious to confer with the LSSAH's commander Mohnke that night. So far Peiper's KG had made a good breakthrough, but where was the rest of the division, much less the entire Ist SS-Panzer Corps?

**December 18**
While most US forces sped out of Stavelot on the night of December 17, the little squad of engineers did get reinforcement, from a company of armored infantry accompanied by TDs. But the new commander bulloxed the situation, ordering antitank mines to be removed from the bridge and a new outpost with 57mm guns set up to its south. When KG Peiper pulled up early in the morning of December 18 they simply blew apart the AT-guns and proceeded into Stavelot. Peiper's breakthrough into the American lines had opened further.

Once through Stavelot, the KG's next objective was Trois Points, which had three bridges, across both the Amblève and the Salm rivers, which met at that town. If Peiper could secure Trois Points he'd finally reach easier terrain and have practically an open field to the Meuse. However, for lack of any other troops, there were still brave US engineers in his way. When Peiper's main column approached north of the Amblève, the engineers blew the bridge in their faces. Two companies of PzKpfw IVs sent directly toward Trois Ponts south of the Amblève saw the Salm bridges blown as soon as the engineers saw them coming. More ominously,

# Dec 18

**Opposite, Above:**
The fuel dump on the Francorchamps road was fired as Peiper's troops got close—although, as it happened, German intelligence had not discovered it.

**Opposite, Inset and Below:**
One of 501st's King Tigers (turret number 105) was abandoned in Stavelot's rue Haut Rivage after backing into a building.

**This Page:**
Trois Ponts was a vital defense point held by 51st ECB. **A** the mouth of the tunnel under the two railway lines from which the LSSAH tanks emerged. At **B** the bridge over the Amblève and memorial (**C**). At **D** the bridge over the Salm. Both these bridges were destroyed in time to friustrate Peiper and force him to head for La Gleize. Peiper later said, "... the enemy blew up the bridge in our faces. If we had captured the bridge at Trois Ponts intact and had had enough fuel, it would have been a simple matter to drive through to the Meuse River early that day."

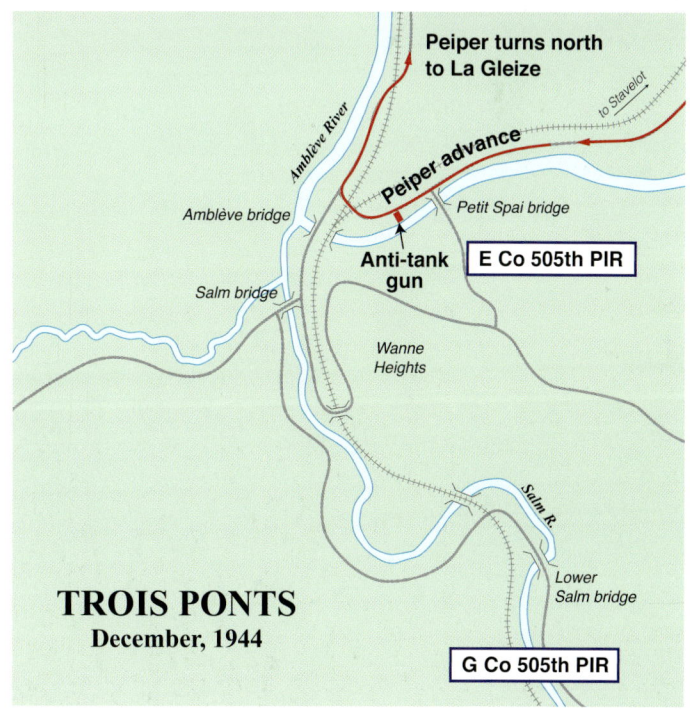

**TROIS PONTS**
December, 1944

33

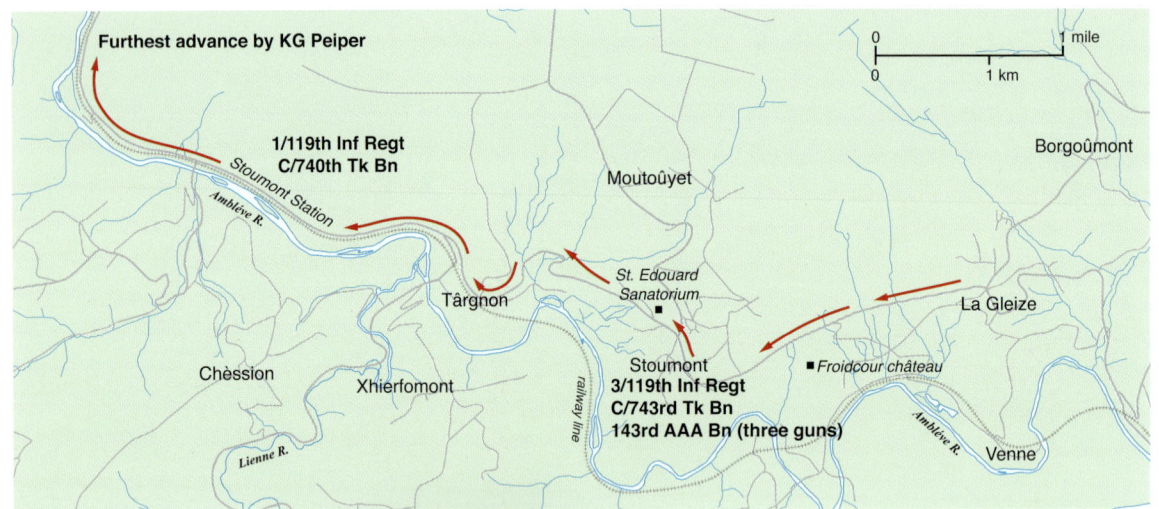

**Above:**
KG Peiper halted at Neufmoulin bridge over the Lienne Creek.

**Left, Below Left, and Below:**
Pushing southwest from La Gleize the Kampfgruppe found the bridge at Cheneux undamaged. However, as they crossed they were hit by fighter-bombers and this Panther was KO'd. Peiper is said to have taken cover in the Belgian pillbox (**Below**) during the attack. The losses were not significant but length of the attack and the time needed to clear the road and get moving again certainly helped the defenders further west. The display board near Peiper's pillbox is one of five linked boards in the area on the theme of the suffering of 1944, each with a wonderful illustration by Philippe Jarbinet.

**Left:** Another of the boards is at Monceau on the heights above Cheneux. Note the Froidcour château in the distance at left.

**Left and Far Left:** One of the crucial moments on December 18 was the blowing of Neufmoulin bridge over the Lienne by "those damned engineers"—the 291st ECB. With this road blocked Peiper was forced to concentrate on the attack at Stoumont. An interesting "what if" is what might have happened had the Operation Greif units—Panzer Brigade 150—been closer to the head of the column than they were. (Peiper disdainfully says in ETHINT 10: "They might just as well have stayed at home, because they were never near the head of the column where they planned to be.") Could they have created sufficient confusion to have take the Neufmoulin—or, indeed, other—bridges?

the PzKpfw IV companies had by now nearly run out of fuel. The main KG was also low, needing resupply. Nevertheless the loss of Trois Ponts was not serious. Peiper could simply follow the Amblève northward and then west to the village of La Gleize, which had its own bridge.

Early in the afternoon Peiper arrived at La Gleize, which was undefended, and began pouring armor over the bridge through the village of Cheneux. But in the otherwise dismal skies during the battle's first week there was suddenly a clearing and waves of P-47 Thunderbolts came racing in. A Panther was knocked out just south of the bridge, and the planes destroyed at least half a dozen other vehicles. More important, the entire column lost two hours as it had to hunker down from the air assaults.

When Peiper finally reached the next water barrier in his path, Lienne Creek, once again US engineers, at the village of Hâbièmont, blew up the bridge in his path. He dispatched recon units up and down the flooded creek to find other crossings and some made it to the other side, only to be shot up by roving US defenders. Peiper ordered a withdrawal back north of the Amblève, leaving behind only a bridgehead garrison at Cheneux. He had meantime been reached by a high-frequency radio which put him in touch with division HQ, and he thus learned

**This spread:**
The crossroads at Kaiserbaracke was the site of a famous series of German Kriegsberichter photos, the film having been captured by the US Army. For many years the left-hand figure in the jeep was said to be Peiper. The King Tiger, number 222, will be seen at various locations on the march. The troops hitching a ride are Fallschirmjäger from I./FJR 9. Today, the area is covered by a business park and there is no meaningful photographic comparison.

that the Americans had closed in behind him at Stavelot.

He would also soon realize that some of the toughest divisions in the US Army were now converging on him. From the south, the 82nd Airborne Division was assembling at Werbomont, after a freezing ride in open-air trucks. From the north, CCB of the 3rd Armored Division had arrived, with attached artillery battalions. And the entire 30th Infantry Division was now on the scene—the unit which after Normandy the propagandist Axis Sally had dubbed "Roosevelt's SS."

# KG Hansen

Max Hansen's Kampfgruppe was nearly as strong as Peiper's, with 4,500 men and 750 vehicles. Except that instead of tanks he had a battalion of 21 Jagdpanzer IV/70s—a good enough cudgel. Hansen had made excellent progress from the start, and after shooting up elements of the US 14th Cavalry and 7th Armored Division's CCR around Poteau, he had broken into the clear on route E, just south of Peiper. It appeared he could drive all the way to Vielsalm on the Salm River, with untold consequences for the US concentration at St. Vith; however, on Dec. 18 orders arrived for him to pause at the village of Recht to wait for the 9th SS-Panzer Division Hohenstaufen to close up. KG Hansen thus spent the entire day of the 19th waiting for a second-wave division to squeeze through the gigantic traffic jams that characterized the army's entire rear area.

Finally given the go-ahead, Hansen reached the Salm at Trois Ponts, to find the 82nd Airborne's 505th PIR had unwisely placed a company on his side of the river as an outpost. Hansen immediately caved it in, and when the 505th's commander sent still another company across, it was sent fleeing also. Panzergrenadiers closed up to the river, even as US paratroopers scrambled down the steep banks and tried to wade or swim to safety. But there was still no way for the Germans themselves to cross at Trois Ponts.

Establishing his HQ at Wanne, Hansen went to the one remaining bridge on the Amblève that remained to the Germans between Stavelot and La Gleize—a small wooden one at Petit Spai that couldn't hold heavy armor. He was still able to get troops across to reinforce Peiper, and the bridge also sustained some back-and-forth traffic in supply and wounded. But even the Petit Spai lifeline came to an end as soon as Hansen was ordered to move his Jagdpanzers across. The very first one that tried crashed the bridge into the river. German engineers, now under heavy artillery fire from north of the Amblève, were unable to fix it.

**Opposite and Below:**
Turning off at Kaiserbaracke (**Opposite, Above Left**) KG Hansen caught CCR of 7th Armored Division near the Poteau crossroads and the famous set of photos shows the aftermath of the engagement on December 18. Today, a roadside marker remembers the incident (**Opposite, Above Right**).

**Bottom and Bottom Left:**
KG Hansen set up its HQ in the chateau at Wanne, where it was joined by Sepp Dietrich. The village was subsequently liberated by the 517th Parachute RCT as shown in the memorial (**Bottom Left**).

# KG Knittel

The smallest of the four Leibstandarte KGs, Knittel's was named a *Schnelle Gruppe* (Fast Group), built around a reconnaissance battalion, and was intended to exploit any breakthroughs to seize bridges over the Meuse in advance of the armor. Originally positioned behind KG Hansen, Knittel vacated that route when Hansen was ordered to pause, and instead directly followed Peiper.

Knittel was able to pass most of his force across the little bridge at Petit Spai, but when he reached Peiper he was ordered to attack back eastward, at Stavelot. The Americans had reoccupied the town, and the vital stone bridge there had to be retrieved. What followed is one of the ugliest chapters of the campaign, as the Americans later found dozens of murdered Belgian civilians, including women and children, in the parts of Stavelot contested by Knittel's men. Earlier, along the Leibstandarte's southernmost route, 11 captured black soldiers of the US 333rd Artillery Bn were also found to be brutally murdered, at the village of Wereth—possibly by Hansen's men but one more suspects Knittel's.

**Top:**
Pallud identifies this as SS-Obersturmführer Goltz (left) and SS-Sturmbannführer Gustav Knittel in Le Vaulx Richard on the 18th. More recent research suggests that it is SS-Obersturmführer Hans-Martin Leidreiter (1920–2007).

**Above:**
Memorial on the Chemin de Chateau, Stavelot, where a halftrack of the 526th AIB was destroyed on December 18. This memorial also commemorates the fallen of the 825th TD Bn, the 30th Inf Div, and the 526th AIB who defended the town.

**Top Left and Right:**
The battle for Stavelot raged on December 19–20. This dead Leibstandarte man lies close to where today one of the Ardennes battlefield markers stands.

**Above and Below:**
The environs of the bridge at Stavelot have changed then and now, but the color palette hasn't. The painting is by US war artist Bernard Arnest.

**Left, Below Left, and Bottom:** Stymied at Hâbiémont with the blowing of the Neufmoulin Bridge, Peiper's Kampfgruppe attacked through Târgnon and Stoumont towards Liege, some 30 miles to the northwest The two WW2 images are stills from a film captured by the Americans and show the attack on Stoumont.

**Opposite, Above:** Peiper's AAA units performed well but often fought an unequal battle against numerous Allied fighter-bomber attacks. This is one of the KG's Wirbelwinds.

**Opposite, Center and Below:** US troops captured in the fighting around Stoumont.

Dec 19

**December 19**

Back at La Gleize, with his KG's vehicles on the verge of running out of fuel, Peiper finally dispatched patrols northward to find the US fuel dumps he knew were in the vicinity of Spa—but these were all beaten back with losses. He nevertheless remained determined to keep driving on to the Meuse, so while parking some of his Panthers in defensive positions at La Gleize, he went onward with a striking force toward the village of Stoumont.

By now significant US forces had arrived from the north and Stoumont was well defended—an armored infantry battalion supported by TDs, as well as 10 Shermans. They could certainly have put up a battle. But the morning of December 19 proved exceptionally foggy, and before the TD crews could even fire, Panzergrenadiers were among them. A US company in the center caved in and its flanking units also had to run. Somehow the 10 Shermans escaped without loss, carrying infantry on their backs, but the Germans took the town as well as 284 prisoners without trouble.

Peiper then decided to lunge for Stoumont Station, a few kilometers beyond, but there it was a different story. At the station the Amblève valley narrowed to only 300 yards, with the river on one side and steep hills on the other, and the Americans had built a wall of firepower to block it. KG Peiper, necessarily having to advance one tank at a time on the road, found itself in a crossfire as soon as its head appeared. Tank after tank was knocked out, and when SS Panzergrenadiers tried to close they

# Dec 20

**Above and Below**
The fighting around Stoumont Station was the farthest point the Kampfgruppe reached. **Below** is the battlefield marker that identifies this spot.

were beaten off. Then US artillery began landing on the German column. Peiper withdrew the probe; it was the farthest he would ever get in the Ardennes campaign.

## December 20

On this day it became clear that Sixth Panzer Army's plan for the offensive had come unraveled. Peiper had made the farthest, fastest breakthrough of any unit, but all he had in support were his fellow Leibstandarte KGs, themselves half-starved for resupply. Dietrich's Sixth Panzer Army had not been able to solve the Ardennes road network, somehow

**Left and Inset:**
The church at Târgnon has a plaque remembering the bravery of the men of 30th Inf Div who liberated the village.

**Bottom and Opposite, Center Right:**
Froidcour Château was used as an aid station for both US and German wounded. Peiper used the lodge as a CP.

**Below:**
KG Peiper, short of fuel, is beaten back by 1/119th Inf Regt.

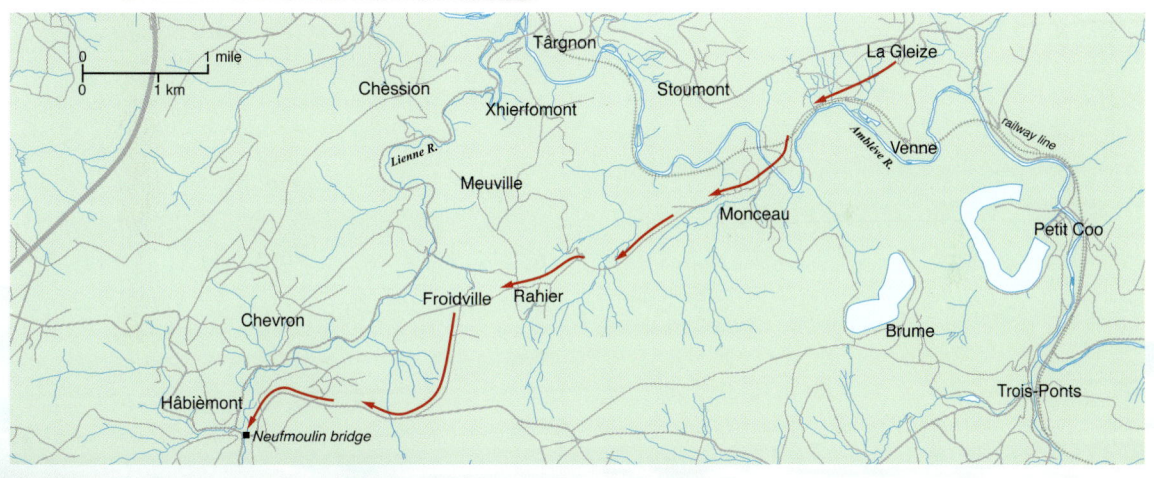

**Above:**
King Tiger 222 (at **1**) was KO'd just south of the bridge over the Amblève at Stavelot.

**Right:**
This aerial view faces south. At **A** the bridge, at **B** the location of the Tiger KO'd on the rue Haut-Rivage (see p. 32); at **C** the main square and battlefield marker; at **D** (and **Below**) the memorial wall next to Stavelot Abbey; at **E** Chemin de Chateau down which Leibstandarte had advanced from the direction of Malmédy; at **F** the road to Trois Ponts that KG Peiper took; at **G** the road to Wanne.

**Below:**
Memorial plaques on a wall (**D**) near Stavelot Abbey. The US hold on Stavelot was crucial. It stopped reinforcements and gasoline reaching the advanced units and tied up forces that could have proved decisive west of Stoumont. Peiper said: "... events turned rapidly against us ... the CO of the reconnaissance battalion reported that Stavelot had been retaken ... On 19 December 1944 ... we began to realize that we had insufficient gasoline to cross the bridge west of Stoumont. Therefore, we ordered the forces west of Stoumont to withdraw to the town." KG Sandig and KG Knittel spent the next few days trying to force a route through Stavelot to open a channel to Peiper's stranded unit, which was about to be counterattacked by CCB 3rd Armored Division, attached to 30th Infantry during December 20. Unfortunately for Peiper, the defenders of Stavelot held firm.

# KG Sandig

congealing itself, even as to the south, Manteuffel's Fifth Panzer Army had leaped division after division onward to the Meuse. Hitler now decided to shift the emphasis of the offensive to Fifth Panzer Army.

Peiper's own follow-up, KG Sandig, had finally arrived at Stavelot, but was defeated in its first, hasty attempt to reclaim the stone bridge. The Germans on the south side and the Americans in the town traded vicious fire across the river, until finally, under cover of a massive artillery barrage, a few daring US engineers rushed forward and blew a gaping hole in the span. So now it was useless. Peiper's remaining hope was that Knittel's men, or Hansen's, could retake the town from the west; but the Americans were getting stronger by the hour and had over 150 artillery pieces zeroed in. Leibstandarte had some 70 south of the river that could answer back, but the US batteries knew better where to aim.

On this day the US plan for the final liquidation of the Leibstandarte's spearhead began to take shape. The

**Top and Above:** 504th PIR marches through Rahier towards Cheneux.

**Opposite, Above:** Cheneux by war artist Harrison Standley.

**Opposite. Below:** Airborne troop movements and advance December 20–25.

three infantry regiments of 30th Infantry Division, supported by CCB of 3rd Armored, divided into three task forces. One to retake Stoumont, another to drive behind La Gleize, and another to hold Stavelot. At the same time the 82nd Airborne would close up to both the Amblève and Salm from below.

The first target of the US paratroopers was the bridgehead Peiper had left behind at Cheneux, across the Amblève from La Gleize. The attack by the 504th PIR, however, turned into a fiasco. The fields outside Cheneux were crisscrossed by barbed wire fences, while German machine guns and Flak vehicles (mounting four 20mm guns) simply raked the approaches. The gallant paratroopers persisted in the confusing, nocturnal attack, only to lose 225 of their number. After bombarding the town the next day, the Americans tried again the following evening. But Peiper had ordered his men to withdraw that evening, as soon as it was dark, so opposition was feeble. The 504th PIR inherited a number of SS vehicles in the town, including 14 of the hated Flak trucks—they were all out of gas.

48

Cheneux

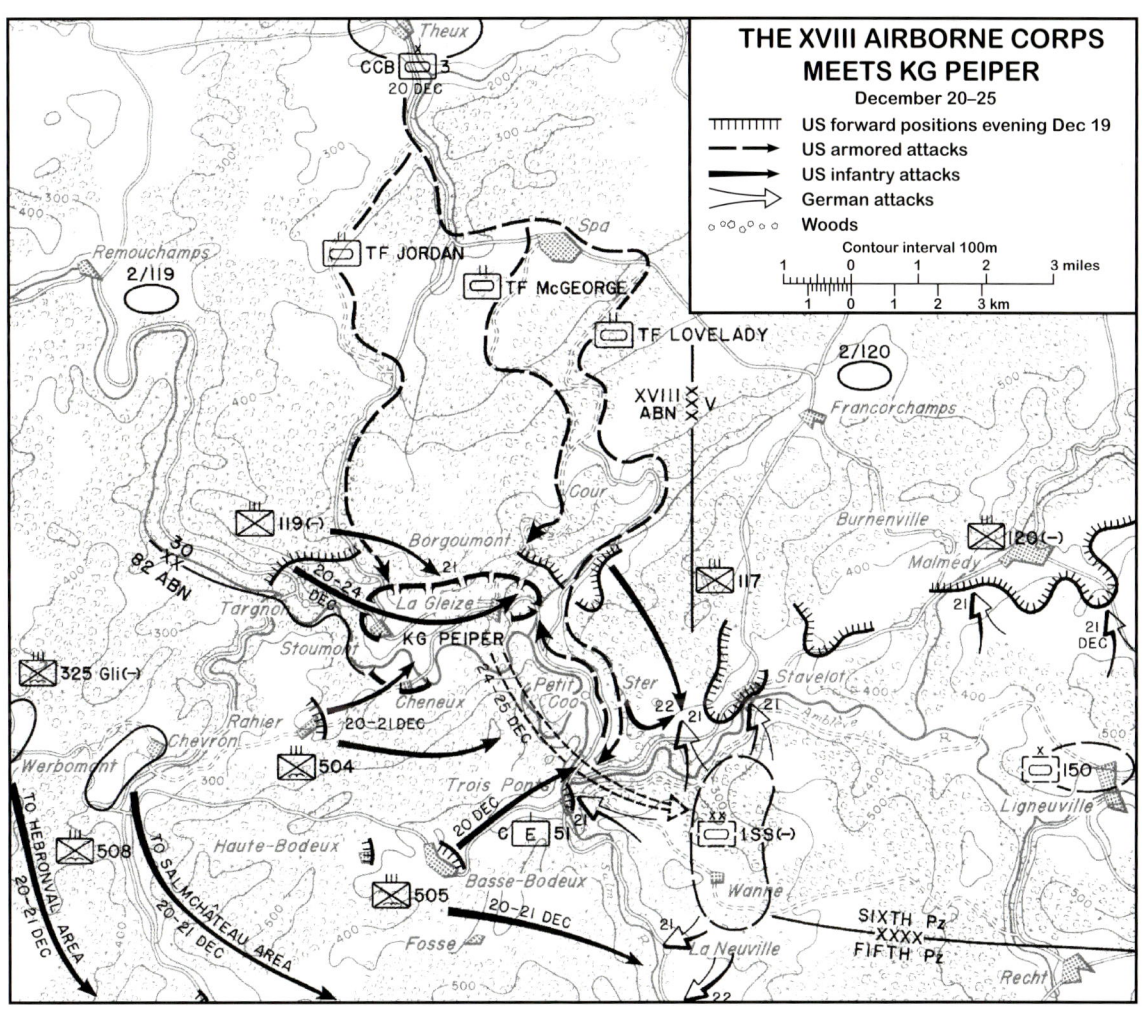

## THE XVIII AIRBORNE CORPS MEETS KG PEIPER
### December 20–25

|  |  |
|---|---|
| ⊥⊥⊥⊥⊥ | US forward positions evening Dec 19 |
| – – → | US armored attacks |
| ⟶ | US infantry attacks |
| ⇒ | German attacks |
| ∘∘∘∘ | Woods |

Contour interval 100m

Coy D, 2/504th PIR talk to the chaplain en route to relieve 1st Bn at Cheneux.

# Dec 21–25

**Below:**
82nd AB bazooka position at Werbomont on December 20.

**Right:**
Memorials at Trois Ponts to 82nd's 505th PIR for its defense of the Salm and for men of 80th AB AAA Bn for the action of December 21.

**December 21–25**

Now that he had withdrawn his bridgehead at Cheneux, Peiper had nothing more to fear from the 82nd Airborne, but he still had the entire 30th Infantry Division, plus CCB 3rd Armored, and all their attached battalions against him north of the Ambleve. With Stoumont untenable and Stavelot lost, there was nothing for it but to hole up in the hilltop village of La Gleize.

First he had to hold back the assaults on Stoumont, however, and the St. Edouard Sanitorium—a large, castle-like building on the west side of town—served as a strongpoint. The furious, close-quarters battle for this building, marked by incredible bravery on both sides, was made more poignant by the 200 civilians who huddled in its basement all the while.

**Above, Left and Right:**
German Panther and artillery piece abandoned in Târgnon.

**Below and Bottom:**
The St. Edouard Sanatorium at Stoumont was the scene of heavy fighting.

**Left and Above:**
The bridge at Petit Spai collapsed under the weight of a Jagdpanzer IV visible at left of photo.

**Below:**
Memorial to the 504th PIR in Cheneux.

December 21 saw the ring on the Leibstandarte closing in, as the Americans pounded Stoumont with artillery throughout the day. When they advanced late in the afternoon they found Peiper had abandoned the place. TF Lovelady, the most dangerous of the 30th Division/3rd Armored Task Forces, had meantime cut the stretch north of the Amblève behind Peiper. The battle for Stavelot was now moot as its bridge had been blown, and the German High Command had shifted the focus of the offensive anyway.

At La Gleize nevertheless, the remnants of KG Peiper retained a good defensive position, and repeated US attacks were repelled. There was nothing to stop the incessant US artillery fire, however, nor the fact that KG Peiper—already out of fuel and soon to be out of ammunition—could not stay there without support.

On December 22 Peiper requested permission to withdraw. Forwarded

52

**Above:**
La Gleize from the Stoumont road, the church at **A** and Town Hall at **B**. KG Peiper repelled a number of attacks before its remnants slipped away on foot, leaving vehicles and wounded behind.

**Right:**
The defense of La Gleize proved effective against US attacks and artillery. A number of Tiger IIs were left after the battle. This is 334 that was sited at Borgoûmont on the northeast of the village.

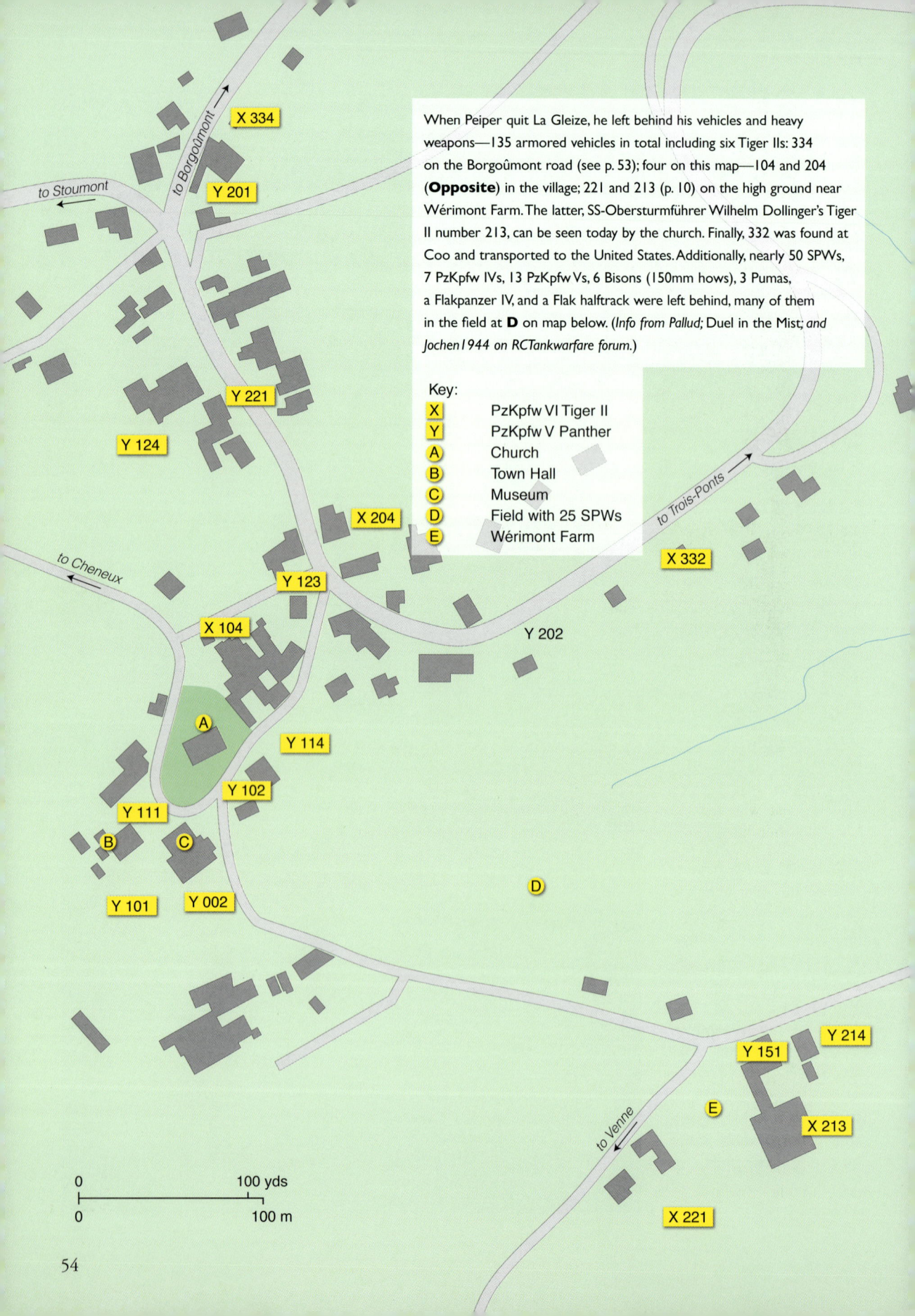

When Peiper quit La Gleize, he left behind his vehicles and heavy weapons—135 armored vehicles in total including six Tiger IIs: 334 on the Borgoûmont road (see p. 53); four on this map—104 and 204 (**Opposite**) in the village; 221 and 213 (p. 10) on the high ground near Wérimont Farm. The latter, SS-Obersturmführer Wilhelm Dollinger's Tiger II number 213, can be seen today by the church. Finally, 332 was found at Coo and transported to the United States. Additionally, nearly 50 SPWs, 7 PzKpfw IVs, 13 PzKpfw Vs, 6 Bisons (150mm hows), 3 Pumas, a Flakpanzer IV, and a Flak halftrack were left behind, many of them in the field at **D** on map below. (*Info from Pallud; Duel in the Mist; and Jochen1944 on RCTankwarfare forum.*)

Key:
- X — PzKpfw VI Tiger II
- Y — PzKpfw V Panther
- A — Church
- B — Town Hall
- C — Museum
- D — Field with 25 SPWs
- E — Wérimont Farm

54

onward to HQ, Sixth Panzer Army, this request was refused. On the 23rd, after another day of enduring incessant artillery fire, and with his men barely holding the perimeter, Peiper again asked for permission to break out. This time the Leibstandarte's division commander, Walther Mohnke, radioed back that the decision could be left to his discretion.

At about 02:00 on Christmas Eve, Peiper's remaining able-bodied troops, numbering about 800, began filing over a wooden foot bridge across the Amblève to the south of La Gleize. Left behind were some lightly wounded men charged with blowing up tanks and other vehicles before the Americans entered the town. Some 300 seriously wounded SS men were also left behind, along with 170 US prisoners. Peiper only took with him a captured US officer, Major Hal McCown of the 30th Inf Div, who escaped during the journey and later testified at Peiper's trial. Evidently a 50-man SS unit on the northern perimeter didn't get the word to withdraw so gave US troops opposition the next day when they moved in.

Meantime the survivors of Peiper's KG made their escape. After a tortuous march behind Trois Ponts, during which they had firefights with units of the 82nd Airborne, Peiper's men were finally able to ford the Salm and reach the village of Wanne, still held by the Leibstandarte's KG Hansen. It was Christmas Day, and a rather pitiful end for the once-mighty KG Peiper, which had originally created such fear as the LSSAH's spearhead.

The American engineers got King Tiger 204 running and drove it toward Roanne-Coo station planning to take it back to the United States. It broke down irredeemably and 332 was taken instead.

**Left, Below Left and Below:**
The central square at La Gleize has changed little since 1944. The Panther and M4 have gone, replaced by a Tiger II; the war memorial has moved to the side.

**Right and Far Right:**
USAAF officers examine the vehicles left behind in La Gleize.

57

**Above and Below**
After the battle, men of the 82nd Airborne test a bazoooka and Panzerfaust against the frontal armor of King Tiger 104. There is similar frontal damage (**Right**) on 213 outside the church.

**Opposite:**
The rail viaduct at Venne and the footbridge over the Amblève crossed by the remnants of KG Peiper as they retreated. The map shows the escape path. Remarkably, 770 out of the 800 who escaped La Gleize reached Wanne. Leibstandarte—without Peiper who was hospitalized—would go on to fight around Bastogne.

59

# Aftermath

**Below:**
There's no getting away from the fact that Leibstandarte's advance into the Ardennes is mired in controversy. They had been linked to atrocities in Poland; as with so many units that had seen action on the Eastern Front, they held the lives of enemy prisoners and civilians cheap. In the Ardennes, there were a number of occasions when atrocities were committed—Malmédy being the best known. Here, Lt Col Hal McCown—captured by LSSAH and confined in cellars in La Gleize—gives his evidence.

**Opposite, Above:**
Artillery bombardments and, often, Allied bombing killed many civilians.

**Opposite, Below Left:**
Memorial to civilian dead at Cheneux.

**Opposite, Below Right:**
Memorial to 9th Armored servicemen murdered at Ligneuville.

Given Hitler's shift of focus in the Ardennes Offensive to Fifth Panzer Army, the SS-Leibstandarte was ordered to regroup east of St. Vith and then move southward to participate in the reduction of Bastogne. There it was pitted against the US 35th Inf Div, as well as elements of the 6th Armored. The German High Command had given up hope of reaching Liege or Antwerp, but the new realization set in that US offensives in the West were paralyzed as long as the Germans kept up their own attack.

On January 10, 1945, the Leibstandarte was ordered to disengage from the Ardennes. It would be needed for a new offensive in the East—as usual built-up and re-equipped in the meantime. But now the walls on the Third Reich were truly closing in, as the Soviets began to move again. Hitler could no longer assemble a serious strategic reserve. The Western gambit, led by Peiper, had been worth playing—but now the room for error had run out.

61

# Cemeteries

**Above:** The Luxembourg American Cemetery and Memorial at Hamm is the resting place for 5,076 service members, many of whom lost their lives in the Battle of the Bulge. Also buried there—with his men— is Gen. Patton.

**Right:** The Henri-Chapelle American Cemetery and Memorial contains the graves of 7,992 US servicemen.

**Left:**
The Ardennes American Cemetery and Memorial at Neupré in Belgium has 5,329 graves. *Romaine/WikiCommons (CC0)*

**Below:**
The main German cemetery in the area of Bastogne is at Recogne, originally a cemetery for both US and German servicemen, it has the graves of 6,807 German soldiers.

# Bibliography

Traces of War (*http://en.tracesofwar.com*) is a fount of knowledge about memorials, fortifications, cemeteries, points of interest, awards.

After Action Report 801st TD Battalion retrieved through Ike Skelton Combined Arms Research Library Digital Library.

Bergstrom, Christer: *The Ardennes 1944–1945*; Vaktel Förlag/Casemate, 2014.

Cavanagh, William C. C., and Karl: *A Tour of the Bulge Battlefields*; Pen & Sword, 2016.

Cooke, David, and Evans, Wayne: *Kampfgruppe Peiper The Race for the Meuse*; Pen & Sword, 2014.

ETHINT 10: "Interview With Joachim Peiper by Major Kenneth W. Hechler," U.S. Army, 1945. Retrieved from *https://www.merriam-press.com/ww2ejour/articles/iss_001/is001_06.htm*

Forty, George: *The Reich's Last Gamble*; Cassel & Co, 2001.

Goldstein, Donald M., Dillon, Katherine V., and Wenger, J. Michael: *Nuts! The Battle of the Bulge The Story and Photographs*; Prange Enterprises Inc, 1994.

Haasler Timm, MacDougall, Roddy, Vosters, Simon, and Weber, Hans: *Duel in the Mist 2*; Panzerwrecks, 2012.

Haasler Timm, Vosters, Simon, and Weber, Hans: *Duel in the Mist 3*; Panzerwrecks, 2014.

King, Martin, Collins, Michael, and Hillborn, David: *The Fighting 30th Division*; Casemate, 1995.

MacDonald, Charles B.: *A Time for Trumpets*; William Morrow, 1997.

Nordyke, Phil: *All American All the Way*; Zenith Press, 2005.

Pallud, Jean Paul: *Battle of the Bulge Then and Now*; After the Battle, 1984.

Reynolds, Michael: *The Devil's Adjutant, Jochen Peiper Panzer Leader*; Spellmount/Sarpedon, 1995.

Sharpe, Michael, & Davis, Brian L.: *Spearhead 5 Leibstandarte*; Ian Allan Ltd, 2002.

USAREUR: *Battle Book The Battle of the Bulge*.

# Key to Map Symbols

**Below:** Sandweiler German war cemetery contains the graves of 10,913 Germans, many of whom died during the Battle of the Bulge.

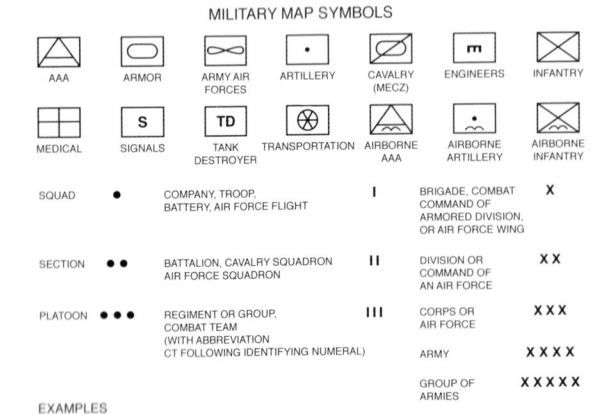